D0444296

HAUNTED SCHOOLS

A.S. Mott

GHOST
HOUSE

Ghost House Books

© 2003 by Ghost House Books
First printed in 2003 10 9 8 7 6 5 4 3 2 1
Printed in Canada

All rights reserved. No part of this work covered by the copyrights hereon may be reproduced or used in any form or by any means—graphic, electronic or mechanical—without the prior written permission of the publisher, except for reviewers, who may quote brief passages. Any request for photocopying, recording, taping or storage on information retrieval systems of any part of this work shall be directed in writing to the publisher.

The Publisher: Ghost House Books

Distributed by Lone Pine Publishing
10145–81 Avenue
Edmonton, AB T6E 1W9
Canada

Website: http://www.ghostbooks.net

National Library of Canada Cataloguing in Publication Data
Mott, Allan, 1975-
  Haunted schools / A.S. Mott.

  ISBN 1-894877-32-2

  1. Ghosts. 2. Haunted places. 3. Schools. I. Title.
BF1461.M67 2003   133.1'22   C2003-910278-5

Editorial Director: Nancy Foulds
Project Editor: Faye Boer
Illustrations Coordinator: Carol Woo
Production Manager: Gene Longson
Cover Design: Elliot Engley
Layout & Production: Lynett McKell
Proofreading: Dori Anne Blackie
Photo Credits: Every effort has been made to accurately credit photographers. Any errors or omissions should be directed to the publisher for changes in future editions. The photographs in this book are reproduced with the kind permission of the following sources: Carol Woo (p. 4-5, 9, 27, 36, 48, 52, 57, 60, 69, 79, 83, 124, 151 178, 181, 186, 197); Julie Woo (p. 122); Getty Images (p. 128); Barbara Smith (p. 134); Library of Congress (p. 171: HABS, NEV, 15-VIRG, 8-1); Roland Lines (p. 188, 191); Toronto Public Library (p. 203; p. 209: T-13106; p. 212: T-13143).

The stories, folklore and legends in this book are based on the author's collection of sources including individuals whose experiences have led them to believe they have encountered phenomena of some kind or another. They are meant to entertain, and neither the publisher nor the author claims these stories represent fact.

We acknowledge the financial support of the Government of Canada through the Book Publishing Industry Development Program (BPIDP) for our publishing activities.

PC: P6

To Bryan Landmann, a teacher

Your school may not be haunted,
but that's only because your students
scared all the ghosts away

CONTENTS

Acknowledgments

I would like thank those who helped me with this book: Faye Boer, my editor, who made this book better than I could have ever dreamed. Chris Wangler for his helpful advice. Dan Asfar and Edrick Thay, my fellow Ghost House writers, who always made themselves available when I needed to ask a question or rant about a false lead, and who always made me feel better by sharing stories of their own difficulties.

I also have to thank Carol Woo for providing the photographs that illuminate this volume and enrich it with a sense of history that prose alone can seldom provide. And I must offer up special kudos to Lynett McKell and Gerry Dotto, whose design contributions make my manuscript look like an actual honest-to-goodness book.

I also have to thank my family, who I didn't thank in my first book and who have since reminded me that without them, I would not exist, making them—in essence—the unremunerated creators of my bibliography.

Finally, I would like to thank Nancy Foulds and Shane Kennedy. Not only did they support me throughout the entire process, but they also paid me. I appreciate that.

Introduction

Let me tell you about one of the first times I came face to face with the power of an urban legend. I was 20 and in my third year of film studies. Wandering around a house party one night I came upon a group of earnest young adults discussing the world of children's entertainment. Having enjoyed the simple charms of *Romper Room*, *Sesame Street* and *Mr. Rogers* all of my life, I felt right at home in joining in.

As we talked, a well-spoken man whom I knew from a drama class said that after Jim Henson died, the people at Sesame Street decided to teach children a lesson about death by giving the popular muppet character Ernie cancer. I said that the story was an urban legend that started as a result of people wondering who would perform Ernie's voice after Jim Henson's shocking and unexpected death. I then explained why the people at *Sesame Street* would never actually do something so controversial, and how it was easy to disprove just by watching a current episode of the show, which inevitably would feature a very-much alive and healthy Ernie. To my surprise, he refused to believe me, proving to me the power of an urban legend. He insisted that he had seen the episode where Ernie died, which was impossible since that episode was never filmed—as proved by film critic Richard Roeper in his book *Hollywood Urban Legends*—but I could tell that he genuinely believed that he had seen the puppet die.

Which brings me to the topic of haunted schools. Given the imagination children possess, it is inevitable that schools are said to be haunted. As a result, when I compiled a list of more than 200 possible schools that I discovered through various contacts, books and websites, I realized that for every well-documented case like those at Galt Collegiate High School, Metz Elementary School or the University of Toronto, there were a dozen stories that required some suspension of disbelief. Some stories, like the ones involving crazed axe-wielding janitors, were obviously the result of imaginative students making up stories to scare their friends or maybe some impressionable younger children. It was easy to dismiss these stories because logic dictated that if a janitor did kill seven students and three teachers and bury their bodies in the boiler room, then it would have made the evening news.

My problem was with the stories that fell in between the two extremes of those that were well documented and above reproach and those that were obviously fictional. For these stories I depended on the thoughts and experiences of others. I had no way to know if what my sources told me was true or was merely the result of the power of an urban legend like the *Sesame Street* story. The more skeptical and cynical of readers may decide to assume the latter, but I decided as I began this project that I wasn't going to try to convince anyone of anything. Instead I felt that it was my duty as a writer to take the stories I found that I felt were most likely to be genuine and present them to you. That is how I would like this book to be judged, by how fun it is to read rather than by how much it confirms whether or not you believe in the supernatural.

1

Haunted
by Accident

No one really thinks about the possibility of sudden death, but the truth is that everyone faces the possibility of death every day. The ghosts in these stories all learned the hard way, and now the schools they once attended are haunted by accident.

Duncan and George

KANSAS STATE UNIVERSITY,
MANHATTAN, KANSAS

Kansas State University, located in the mid-sized town of Manhattan, is home to 24 fraternities. Among these 24 Greek brotherhoods are organizations that manage to be as diverse as they are similar, differing in the makeup of their members and pledges, but alike in the pride that they take in their history. And it is in history that we so often find links to the supernatural. A quick study of paranormal activity on campuses throughout North America shows that many ghost stories involving higher education take place not in classrooms or lecture halls, but in fraternities. There are three reasons why. The first is that fraternities are more likely to be aware of the history of the places they live in and of the people who lived there. The second is that the buildings that house fraternities are frequently old, and the third is that the young men who join and live in fraternities are usually predisposed to drinking enormous quantities of beer. The final reason alone accounts for many campus ghost stories, but among these alcohol-induced tall tales, there are a handful of stories that strike those who study the paranormal as being the real deal.

Today, thanks to movies such as *National Lampoon's Animal House* and *Revenge of the Nerds*, many people believe that belonging to a fraternity is simply an excuse to indulge in sophomoric pranks and wild debauchery. In fact, many young men pledge fraternities every year for exactly that reason, and are often chagrined to discover that, along with the pranks and the parties, they are expected to help out local charities and even, on occasion, study. More than keggers and beer blasts, belonging to a fraternity means having a group of people around you who understand what you are going through and who are willing to help you get through it. The cost of joining, though, is more than simply an annual fee. Pledges are expected to prove their worthiness by undergoing a series of tests and humiliations known as hazing; a trial by fire designed to weed out the wannabes from the genuine articles. Today a pledge is more likely to face personal embarrassment during his week of initiation, than he is physical violence, but years ago it wasn't uncommon for him to prove his worth through pain. Almost all fraternities have stopped this practice of torture, thanks to the shocking nights when these tests proved accidentally fatal.

The frat house on the Manhattan street of 1716 Fairchild has been home to three different fraternities over the past 50 years. Each one has had to deal with the aftermath of a hazing that went horribly wrong in the late 1950s. Duncan was a young man who decided to pledge Theta Xi, because of its emphasis on academics. Along with several other pledges, he made it through hell week and found himself in the Theta Xi living room, awaiting what would be his final test. Like so many other fraternities, Theta Xi employed the use of a ceremonial paddle during its final initiation ritual. A pledge was expected to take five hard whacks on his posterior before he could be welcomed as a brother. The severity of the test depended greatly on the temperament of the person holding the paddle. It was the job of the Theta Xi president to deliver the blows, and he alone decided how much pain to inflict. Some presidents were sadistic, while others were kind.

Duncan was last in the line of pledges bent over to receive their blows. From the shouts and oaths of the others in front of him, it became clear that this year wasn't going to be a good one to be a pledge. The current president was putting all of his weight and the full force of his strength into his swings. Duncan was not a physically brave person. He feared pain in the way many people fear heights or deep water. As the president made his way down the line, Duncan began to perspire nervously and his stomach began to cramp up from the tension. Finally, the president made his way to the boy beside Duncan. Knowing that he was next was too much for Duncan to take and he jumped up just as the president swung back the paddle to deliver the blow. The speed with which Duncan sprang up and the force of the president's back swing proved an unfortunate combination. The paddle struck Duncan on the head, and he fell to the ground in an unconscious heap. By the time he got to the hospital, he was dead.

Chastened by the accident, Theta Xi retired the paddle that had killed the young pledge and hung it on the wall to honor his memory. It stayed there for a decade until the frat house was purchased in 1968 by the Phi Gamma Deltas (known around campus as the Fijis). As members of Theta Xi packed up, they took down the paddle and were shocked to discover that a dark shadow lingered on the wall in its place. The Fijis moved in and painted the wall on which the paddle's shadow remained. But the shadow bled through the paint. They painted over it again, but the shadow remained visible. They tried a few more times before they decided to give up, and they covered the wall with paneling.

In 1993 Pi Kappa Phi bought the house from the Fijis and almost immediately took down the paneling on the haunted wall. The shadow was still there. Like the Fijis, they tried everything to cover it up. Finally, it was only after the room was completely remodeled that they were able to get rid of it. After that some Pi Kappa Phis reported hearing the sound of phantom footsteps and seeing flickering lights and doors opening on their own, suggesting to some that, having lost his place on the wall, Duncan had returned to the frat house in a more substantial form.

Pi Kappa Phi is not the only fraternity house from Kansas State to claim a ghost. Delta Sigma Phi also has a phantom in its midst, although considerably more eccentric than Duncan. Known only as George, he is a remnant of the time when the Delta Sigma Phi house was a hospital. George was an elderly patient at St. Mary's who died after he accidentally rolled off his bed and became tangled in his sheets, where he slowly suffocated. As bizarre and unfortunate as the accident was, it wasn't enough to damper the spirits of the gregarious George, who was always happiest when he was helping people, a trait that stayed with him even after death.

When the fraternity moved into the old hospital, a few boxes were accidentally dropped and the clocks they contained were broken. No longer of any use, the clocks were thrown in a corner and forgotten, until one day a Delta

Sigma Phi brother decided to throw them out. To his surprise he discovered that the clocks now seemed to be working. It was as if they had simply fixed themselves.

After a series of other similar incidents, the fraternity did some research about the house and decided that George was the person most likely to be their phantom repairman. Although no one has ever seen George, it became apparent in 1973 that he could often be found in front of the television, and that his favorite show was one that didn't start airing until after his death.

That year there was a nasty ice storm in Manhattan that caused blackouts almost everywhere. The frat house was plunged into darkness and the brothers were forced to improvise increasingly juvenile ways to pass the time. To their relief, at 4 PM the lights came back on and everybody ran to the TV to watch their favorite afternoon rerun, *Star Trek*. After they enjoyed the episode, the TV set shut itself off along with all of the lights. The power seemed to be off again. The blackout continued into the next day, until, once again, the lights came back on at 4 PM. After *Star Trek* was over, everything shut off again. That state of affairs went on for a week, until finally all the power was returned to the neighborhood. As strange as it seemed, the only explanation for the bizarre phenomenon was that George really liked *Star Trek* and he used his own power to get the electricity working for the one hour every day that the show came on.

Duncan and George are just two of the many frat house ghosts said to exist in North America, but their stories are unique and are too much a part of their fraternity's history to be dismissed as phantoms concocted only after the brothers drank too many spirits. While tequila-shot ghost stories aren't uncommon, their loose ends and cheap dramatics easily identify them. These two stories avoid those flaws and are therefore worthy of our attention.

Burnt to Hell

LAMBERTVILLE HIGH SCHOOL, LAMBERTVILLE, NEW JERSEY

In the paranormal community it isn't uncommon for a place to earn a reputation for its strange and eerie atmosphere. In much the same way that some people go to fashionable restaurants, supernatural enthusiasts will often descend on these spooky sites in packs, not because they believe they'll actually see something but because it's too embarrassing to admit that they haven't been there yet. On a deserted hilltop in the town of Lambertville, New Jersey, there sits an abandoned schoolhouse that over the years has become one of these sites of paranormal interest.

Built in 1855, the Lambertville High School was originally a cozy-looking red brick schoolhouse that had been transformed through two fires into a dangerous and frightening structure. Charred, twisted and marred by decades of vandalism and disuse, it isn't hard to understand why people who are interested in the unknown feel compelled to travel from all around North America to visit it. In fact, interest in the old wreck is such that a popular supernatural website named www.lostdestinations.com actually sells T-shirts and other items with the school's name on them. Included on the T-shirts is a nod to the graduating class of 1927, the class most affected by the school's first fire that gutted its halls in 1926.

According to local history, no one died in the 1926 fire, but when the inside of the school was remodeled, it was said to have taken on a much darker and heavier atmosphere. Many assumed that it was a negative consequence of the cheap and quick repair job, but others felt that it had less to do with the new interior than with the violence of the flames. These people believed that the fire had a disastrous effect on the school's spiritual energy, darkening it forever and turning it into a lightning rod for evil forces.

It was after the 1926 fire that the legend of Buckeye began to take hold at the school. An urban legend, similar to the type referred to in the popular *Candyman* film series, Buckeye's story, like many of its ilk, was inspired by an actual event, when a young football player named Billy Scrimshaw was killed during a football game. Billy, whose nickname was Buckeye, was a powerful quarterback with an arm that today would earn him millions of dollars even before he turned 20. Back then it was good enough to make him one of the most popular boys at the school, despite his natural shyness.

In an age when handholding was frowned upon because of what it could lead to, Billy was considered by some to be too conservative. It came then as a huge surprise when he started to court a pretty schoolmate named Maria Di Novi. It was shocking because Maria was a Catholic and Billy was a strict Baptist, and because Maria was also being wooed by Billy's teammate and the school's other quarterback, Norman Fancher. For the first time in Billy's life, he felt inclined to loosen his strong moral code so that he could pursue the object of his romantic affections. Billy's actions enraged Norman, who for the past year had planned to propose to Maria as soon as they graduated. Maria, for her part, couldn't help but take some pleasure in being chased by her school's two most popular boys and did little to indicate whom she liked more.

Finally, Norman couldn't take it anymore and he challenged Billy to a game of football that would decide who got to see Maria. Billy agreed, and they met on a Saturday morning at the football field. They were joined by almost the entire student body, and it was from them that the two suitors chose the players to make up their teams. Other students were drafted to serve as officials, and the game started. They had decided on a one-hour time limit and the score was tied at 14–14 after 55 minutes of play. Neither Norman or Billy had any intention of losing, and both decided that in these last five minutes they would do whatever they had to do to keep the other team from scoring.

Norman's team had the ball and was at the 40-yard line. Norman wasn't as accurate a thrower as Billy was, but his arm was just as strong and he could easily score points from his position. To do so, he had decided to try a fake and sneak the ball over to Dennis Klayman, who, he had observed, was being ignored by Billy's team during the past five minutes. What he didn't know was that Billy had told his teammates to ignore Dennis for exactly that reason. Billy knew that he was faster than Dennis was and that he could rush in front of him to make an important interception. The play started and Billy's team allowed Norman to think that he had faked them out by running towards his seemingly intended target. Norman then rocketed the ball as hard as he could towards Dennis. Billy couldn't help but smile as he ran towards Dennis and got in front of the ball. But his smile vanished when, instead of falling into his hands as he had envisioned, the ball smashed into his face. Billy crumpled and his body fell to the ground with a sickening thud. Everyone rushed over to him and their worst fears were instantly confirmed. He was dead. The force of Norman's throw had been so great that it was enough for the football to snap Billy's neck.

Decades passed and the incident was seldom mentioned at the school, until the fire caused the somber darkness that overtook it. After that students began to insist that if anyone stood at the staircase where Norman originally challenged Billy and shouted out "Hey Buckeye, do you want a game?" the last thing they would see would be a football hurtling at neck-breaking speed towards their head. Though a few brave souls were able to prove that the assertion was patently absurd, many people, to this day, refuse to invoke Billy's nickname while they tour the lifeless school.

Many who feel compelled to visit what used to be Lambertville High, which was abandoned in the 1950s and suffered its second fire in 1992, do so armed with the very best photographic gear they can afford. Even though they are certainly interested in the school's dilapidated architecture, that isn't the reason they choose to lug around expensive equipment. Pictures of orbs, the shining balls of light that many believe to be aimless spirits, are what they are after, and they are seldom disappointed. For whatever reason, these skittish balls of light seem to be attracted to the empty school and it only requires a bit of luck and patience to capture them on film. That is, if you can get your camera to work. On the Lost Dimensions website, an orbhunter who refers to himself as Shady describes how the brand-new batteries he had just put into his camera completely drained of power almost as soon as he stepped into the building. Luckily his partner's camera still managed to work and they were still able to get some photos. Another strange photographic phenomenon at the school is the way that pictures of certain markers and landmarks rarely develop properly. Blurring, overexposure or some other photographic mishap almost always mar pictures of these icons.

Although the cause of these occurrences and the identity of the men and women whose souls flit about as balls of golden light are still unknown, it hasn't stopped people who are fascinated by the paranormal from raving about the abandoned building once known as Lambertville High School. They are simply happy that it exists and allows them to explore a world and feeling that is so hard to come by in everyday life. If it is true that darkness took over the school after the first fire in 1926, then maybe the school's second fire in 1992 drove that darkness out and allowed it once again to become a place that people want to be near. Whatever the case, this much is true—if you're going to be in New Jersey, you should check it out.

Art Attack

Almost everyone in North America has at one time or another heard of California's San Andreas fault line, the strip of land beneath the Earth's surface whose unpredictable movements cause the earthquakes that plague the state. Not nearly as many people have heard of the New Madrid fault line that starts in Arkansas and ends in Missouri. The San Andreas fault is much more active than the New Madrid and causes powerful earthquakes on a regular basis. New Madrid's quakes, on the other hand, are barely detectable. However, the frightening truth is that if and when the New Madrid does cause a massive quake, its effects could cause 10 times the damage of the San Andreas. Because of the length of the fault and because the soil in the central United States is much looser and sandier than on the west coast, it would serve as a much more powerful conductor of destructive shock waves.

A New Madrid earthquake of a scale similar to those experienced in California could have devastating effects in Arkansas, Indiana, Missouri, Illinois, Kentucky, Mississippi and Tennessee. Luckily the worst quake ever to be caused by the New Madrid fault occurred in 1811, when those states were still sparsely populated. Registering around a 9.0 on the Richter scale, the 1811 quake temporarily caused the Mississippi River to reverse its course and even formed new lakes. Today, an earthquake of that scale would inevitably cause a human disaster unlike any ever experienced before in American history. In 1899, just a small tremor was powerful enough to destroy the Catherine Spalding Elementary School in Owensboro, Kentucky. Two young girls died in the wreckage and their spirits have remained over the years in the spot where they died.

Built in 1896, the small school was meant to educate young boys and girls, but in the rural town of Owensboro most of the boys were needed to work on the family farms, so the majority of the school's students were female. Two of these girls, Virginia Union and Isabelle Benton, were best friends who lived on neighboring farms. They were 10 years old when classes started and had vivid imaginations that they expressed through their love of arts and crafts. Ginia and Izzy, their nicknames for each other, often got into trouble because whenever their teacher looked at the work they were supposed to be doing on their slates, she would usually find a drawing instead of a math equation or a properly parsed sentence.

But both of the girls still did well in their classes, and in 1899 were, at the age of 13, close to graduating from grade six. Both dreamed that they would someday leave their farms and move to New York or Europe where they would become a part of the exciting world of the artistic bonhomie, but their dreams were extinguished when a minor shock wave caused by the New Madrid fault hit their small town. The students were at work on some math problems their teacher had written on the board when the whole building began to shake violently. It happened so suddenly that there was no time to evacuate. Everyone jumped down under their desks as the ceiling toppled down onto them. The ground still shook and the students cried as the dust seared their lungs and the debris cut into their flesh. Finally, the tremor ended and most of the students were able to lift themselves out of the rubble. Luckily for them, their desks bore the brunt of the collapsed roof and saved their lives. Their teacher, who was understandably upset by what had just happened, calmed herself and did a head count. She found that five students were unaccounted for. With the help of some of the older students she worked her way through the wreckage and found the missing children. Three had been knocked unconscious, but were still breathing. That just left Izzy and Ginia. Their desk had sat directly under the ceiling's heaviest support beam, which fell and crushed the desk they shared, killing them instantly. They were the tremor's only casualties.

Two years later, in 1901, the school was rebuilt. Although it remained a plain one-story building, the new version of the school was larger and had several different rooms, including one designed to be an art classroom. For the first few years the art room wasn't used that often, but as the local farmers became more concerned about education for their sons, the student population doubled and the need for the room greatly increased. Eventually the classroom became equipped with everything a young artist could ever desire—paint, pencils, modeling clay, crayons—and it soon became evident that some students were enjoying the use of these items when they weren't supposed to.

One day after school, a staff member spent an hour cleaning up the room before she left for the day, only to come back in the morning to find that nothing was where she had put it. She asked her co-workers if anyone had moved anything and was told no by everyone, so she assumed it was the work of some mischievous students. She returned the items to their proper places and left the school as she had the night before. But, hoping to catch the students in the act, she waited outside the school and returned to the room a half-hour later. What she found caused her mouth to hang open in shocked amazement. The room was a mess. Not only was nothing where she had just put it, but it appeared that whoever had been in there had started some sort of project. But the room was empty. She searched the school and found no one. There was no way anyone could have gotten away like that.

These inexplicable incidents happened several times as the years went on, and during that time no one could figure out who was sneaking into the art classroom and using the supplies. Despite several attempts at stakeouts, no one was ever caught entering or exiting the room during the times when these incidents occurred. Sometimes the culprits would clean up after themselves, and sometimes they would just leave a mess. Eventually, someone suggested that the cause might be supernatural in nature. It was then that someone remembered the two girls who had died when the original school collapsed. As bizarre as it sounded, the most reasonable explanation for what was happening seemed to be that the spirits of Izzy and Ginia couldn't resist playing with all of the wonderful art supplies the school now offered. A possible explanation for why the mysterious artists sometimes left a mess is because someone interrupted them. Not wanting to bring attention to themselves, they had no choice but to leave everything where it was. They put everything away, albeit in the wrong places, only when they were able to finish what they working on.

The great mystery to this story, however, is what the two young girls do with the projects they work on. No one has ever found a piece of art that could be attributed to the ghosts, causing many to doubt the veracity of the haunting. Those who do believe have two theories about why no known examples of the girls' work exist. The first is that the girls have found a place, as yet undiscovered, to hide their work, and the second is that the girls aren't actually able to create anything, but they enjoy being able to play with the wonderful supplies.

Of these two theories, it is the former that one hopes is true. Given the completely random and unexpected way in which Izzy and Ginia died, it feels good to believe that their spirits are still somehow able to do the one thing they loved more than anything, create art. Maybe someday the New Madrid fault will cause another minor shock wave and the earth will open up and expose a hidden gallery of never-before-seen art projects.

A Walking Disaster

ST. FRANCIS XAVIER UNIVERSITY, ANTIGONISH, NOVA SCOTIA

In 1894, a small Catholic women's school named St. Bernard's Academy in Antigonish, Nova Scotia, joined together with the small town's Catholic school for men, St. Francis Xavier University, and was renamed Mount St. Bernard College. Just three years after the union of the two schools, St. Francis Xavier University became the first Catholic university to grant degrees to women in North America. It was thanks to the then-controversial decision that scores of Catholic women flocked to the Maritime school, where they found a college whose façade betrayed its humble origins. The halls that made up Mount St. Bernard were square and unadorned, bearing few of the architectural flourishes that usually distinguish a school's buildings. As well as students, the college was also home to a small convent and for that reason the school's décor was simple and plain. A hundred years later little has changed. Students have made it their business to make the school's interiors less drab, but the exteriors are still prime examples of the no-frills aesthetic and give little hint of the supernatural thrills that they have become a home to.

There are many ghosts at Mount St. Bernard. They come in all shapes and sizes. Many are nameless and many are formless, appearing only as sounds, cold spots and uncomfortable feelings of something a person can't describe. They appear everywhere at the college, but a few places are more haunted than others.

As a woman walks up and down the spiral staircase, she is apt to feel as though a pair of eyes has descended upon her, and if she looks quickly she might catch a glimpse of the ghost who has haunted the stairs for over 75 years. Once a student at St. Francis Xavier, the man who came to haunt the staircase was infamous for trying to get into rooms that were off limits to men. Those closed doors were coals in the fire of his imagination, and when he was finally expelled for entering them once too often, he continued to hang around the college, where he stared at the women with a look of disconcerting intent. Eventually the authorities were informed and the man was dealt with. No one saw him alive after that. Five years after he left, the women at the school once again felt themselves the uncomfortable focus of his ogling eyes, but this time there was nothing anyone could do. Somehow the man had died and his spirit returned to Mount St. Bernard and took up residence on the spiral staircase that all the students eventually had to climb. But now that all he can do is look, his behavior is more rude than frightening.

Mount St. Bernard's leering phantom was quite possibly one of the reasons an elevator was installed in the college, but it too has become possessed by a playful spirit. Unlike the staircase stalker, the fun-loving ghost prefers to avoid the presence of others and plays its favorite game all by itself. Late at night this mischievous spirit rides up and down the elevator, stopping at each floor as it does. No one knows whose spirit is so enamored with the modern convenience, but at least it keeps its pleasures simple and leaves everyone alone.

Also nameless and faceless are the spirits that can be heard walking through the school halls late at night, talking to each other, flushing toilets in the bathrooms and casting dark shadows that float across the walls. Who they are and why they haunt the school are questions that only create more questions. No one can even figure out how many different ghosts there are. It is possible after all that just a few are responsible for all the noise and shadows, but then it is equally possible that for each strange occurrence there is only one specific ghost responsible, which could add up to dozens.

One of the few whose story is known is the ghost who haunts the balcony at Gilmora Hall, one of the college's residences. Known as Mary, this apparition is the spirit of a former student who was known for her clumsiness. Able to trip over a shadow, she was the cause of several accidents and mini-disasters, including one incident in which she upended a table covered with food. The natural human impulse would be to avoid someone as accident-prone as Mary, but her fellow students were actually in awe of her. In all other respects she was a blessed person, smart and beautiful with a talent for art and literature. Instead of fleeing from her, her peers couldn't help but follow her so they could witness her next catastrophe. If Mary ever noticed the undue attention, she never acknowledged it. In fact she didn't even seem to be aware that trouble was always only seconds away from wherever she went. She just assumed that everyone wrote as many apology notes as she did. As amusing as her clumsiness was, it finally turned tragic when Mary's almost mystical clumsiness caused her death.

It was a warm autumn night and Mary decided to spend it on the Gilmora Hall balcony, with a book and a bag of peanuts. Despite, or maybe because of, her gift for destruction, she was a habitually neat person and was careful about depositing the peanut's shells into the paper bag she had brought with her for just that purpose. When the sun began to set Mary decided to go back to her room and got up to leave. As she stood up her foot stepped on the one tiny part of a peanut shell that she had failed to get inside the paper bag. It caused her to slide back, but she managed to avoid falling by grabbing hold of the wooden chair she had been sitting on. Unfortunately, the chair was old and it snapped in half, propelling Mary headfirst into the wall beside it. Dazed, Mary tried to stand up straight, but her dizziness caused her to stumble backwards into the balcony railing. Before she knew what was happening, she flipped over the railing and fell to her death to the ground below. It all happened in a few seconds.

Ever since then, Mary's spirit has been a presence on the balcony. Those who have seen her ghost have described it as looking both cross and confused, which isn't hard to believe. After all the near misses in Mary's star-crossed life, it seemed as though fate had a most ridiculous end in store for her.

The ghosts of St. Francis Xavier University's Mount St. Bernard College are an intriguing collection of the disconcerting, the comical, the playful, the creepy and the unknowable. Although none is so bothersome that they disturb the students, they are still active enough to never be forgotten.

The Shop Teacher

LIVONIA CHURCHILL HIGH SCHOOL, LIVONIA, MICHIGAN

If you were to ask any of his students, not a single one would describe Mr. Fairfax as being the romantic sort. As the shop teacher at Livonia Churchill High School in Michigan, he had a reputation as a take-no-prisoners and always-expect-the-best teacher whom students simultaneously feared and respected. He ruled his classes like a drill instructor, but with enough of a sense of humor that he didn't become a joke like some other teachers. Instinctively, his students understood that he acted this way because, unlike any of the other classrooms, his offered up a great variety of ways for students to mangle and mutilate themselves. Mr. Fairfax couldn't tolerate any monkey business because in shop class, monkey business could get a person killed. To him his job was not to teach his students how to work with tools and build things with their own hands, but to show them the virtues of discipline and a constant self-awareness. But despite his gruff exterior, inside Mr. Fairfax was a man who truly adored the woman to whom he had been married for 17 years, and it was his hidden romantic nature that caused him to forget his own lessons and suffer a fate almost diabolical in its irony.

Mr. Fairfax, or Wayne as he was known to anyone over the age of 17, had been stumped for the past three months trying to think of an anniversary present for his wife, Beth. Last year he had surprised her by finding a ring that looked exactly like one her grandmother had once owned and that she had always admired. He had never before seen her so surprised and happy. She had cried and hugged him and had told him that it was the most wonderful present she had ever received from anyone. Seeing her like that was more than worth all the time and money he had spent trying to find the ring. But as their next anniversary edged closer, he began to worry when he realized he had no idea how he was going to top last year's gift. He knew that Beth would be happy with whatever he gave her, even if it was just a card, but he wanted to relive that moment of joy that had kept him so happy over the past year.

Since he wanted it to be a surprise, he couldn't simply ask her what she might want, so he listened carefully to every random comment she made in the hope that it would offer up a clue. His attentiveness proved successful when, as they watched a nature documentary on TV, Beth started talking about how her uncle used to have a big birdhouse in his backyard and how she used to love sitting in front of it and watching the birds come and go. Wayne pretended to listen politely, while his heart raced with excitement. He knew what he was going to give her.

But his was not going to be an average birdhouse. After nearly two decades of seeing student after student churning out the small aviary domiciles, he knew the wheat from the chaff. He was going to build the Taj Mahal of birdhouses. Its beauty would be unparalleled, and people would drive from out of state just to say they had seen it.

The problem was that he had only two months to create his masterpiece and somehow get it done without

Beth finding out about it. Carefully, with the discipline and self-awareness that he taught so successfully to his students, he came up with a design and a schedule that would allow him to get the job done. Every Tuesday, Beth went out with friends, and on Thursdays she took a pottery class, so that gave Wayne two evenings a week when he could slip into his classroom and construct his birdhouse without arousing suspicion. With eight weeks to go until the big day, that gave him 16 days. The first seven weeks went off without a hitch and he managed to remain on schedule, but on the Tuesday that marked the second to last day that he had to work on it, Beth, in preparation for next week's anniversary, decided to stay home and get romantic. Wayne did his best not to seem anxious as she prepared them a lovely dinner and put on some gentle music. But all he could think about was that he had to cut and sand the front façade of the birdhouse before he could paint it and attach it to the completed body. Beth noticed her husband's look of concern and asked him what was wrong. Not wanting to give anything away, Wayne just smiled and insisted that everything was fine.

As they went to bed that night, a knot of worry began to twist in Wayne's stomach. Thursday was the only evening he could go to the school and finish the birdhouse, but he was afraid that there wasn't going to be enough time to finish.

It was because of his fear that, when Thursday night arrived, he abandoned safety measures in order to get the job done. He'd taught his students every day that there was never any excuse to rush a project if it meant endangering yourself but, in his haste, he ignored his own lessons.

All it took was a single second's loss of concentration for his hand to slip as he operated the band saw. It happened too quickly for him to feel any pain, so he was shocked when he looked down and saw his severed hand. Seconds later he lost consciousness and fell to the floor. When he was found, he had bled to death.

Wayne's intentions were nothing but good, but his desire to recreate a wonderful moment in his and Beth's life together resulted only in her becoming a grieving widow. The birdhouse was never finished, and that may be the reason why Mr. Fairfax's spirit returned to the classroom where he died.

Within weeks of his death, the cleaning staff began to report that the shop's machinery turned itself on and off at night. Though strange, what made it stranger was that these incidents seemed to occur only on Tuesdays and Thursdays. It was clear that the ghost of Wayne Fairfax was intent on completing the project that took his life. Unfortunately, the form his spirit has taken only seems to allow him to turn on the machinery, but not operate it. Livonia Churchill High School's ghost is caught in a catch-22—it can only leave the school's shop when the birdhouse is finished, but it cannot work with the tools that will get the job done. Another obstacle in the phantom's path is that the only piece of machinery to never turn itself on is the band saw. Apparently, Wayne's ghost is too afraid of the tool that killed him to go near it, and without the band saw, the job will never be completed.

It is a sad irony that such a good teacher should be forced to spend his afterlife forever stuck in the classroom where he taught because of one moment when he chose not to follow his own important rules. Especially considering that the reason for his recklessness was his desire to make his wife happy. Perhaps the lesson here is that a person should not place so much importance in recreating the past. There are some moments that simply cannot be relived, and it is foolish to risk everything so you can feel all those same emotions again.

Roberta's Choice

NORTHWEST MISSOURI STATE UNIVERSITY, MARYVILLE, MISSOURI

Sometimes people don't want to die. No matter how badly they suffer, they still insist on clinging to this mortal coil because of the fear of the unknown. Having fought so long and hard to stay on this earth, these spirits insist on returning, choosing to ignore the strange new possibilities of the "undiscovered country." These ghosts of the unwillingly deceased are often the most unpredictable of spirits. One moment they can offer up a radiant benevolence, lovingly looking out for the people they left behind, and then in the next fly into a rage, angrily protesting the cruel injustice of their fate. In a dormitory at Northwest Missouri State University in Maryville, Missouri, there exists just such a ghost. After an accident in 1951, Roberta Steel lingered with her injuries for six months before she finally succumbed to them. After the briefest tours of what comes after death, she returned to this world, and after 50 years, she still cannot let go.

Roberta was a cheerfully homely girl with a big round face and small sleepy eyes. We have the impression of a shy girl, who nonetheless made every effort to be friendly and outgoing. Although she had just begun her studies and wasn't sure what she was going to do with them, she might have become an excellent schoolteacher or a loving mother, which, given the era in which she lived, were likely her two best options. But as she sat in her dorm room at NWM State one warm night in April, a sudden disturbance rendered all of her options void.

It was April 28 and Roberta was studying. Not one to enjoy silence, she had set her desk up by her window and always kept it open so she could listen to the sounds of nature and campus life outside. She heard birds singing, students talking and the sounds of leaves rustling in the wind. Instead of distracting her, these sounds wrapped around her like a cocoon and made it easier for her to concentrate on her textbook. The calm she felt made it impossible for her to react immediately to the thunderous blast that rocked the campus and could be heard throughout Maryville. In Roberta's case, however, even if she had reacted immediately, it still would not have been soon enough. A burst of flame shot through her window and surrounded her, changing her life forever.

Below her window at the south wing of the building, a propane tank had exploded. The force of the blast had thrown the tank 100 feet into the air and blew out many of the windows in the surrounding buildings. The first and second floors of the dorm were engulfed in flame and besides Roberta, four other students were seriously injured. They were all rushed to St. Joseph's Hospital and treated for severe burns. Of the five unlucky students, Roberta was the worst off; she had third-degree burns all over her face and body.

It wasn't uncommon for people as badly burned as she to expire from the pain alone. Roberta, though, refused to give in to the pain. By November 29 the constant war she had battled against her own body had so exhausted her that she was unable to defend herself any longer. She died.

The only student to die as a result of the accident, Roberta was honored by the university when it renamed the dorm in which she had lived Roberta Hall. Not long afterwards the young women who lived inside the hall began to notice strange occurrences. Doors and windows would lock and unlock themselves and lights turned themselves off. At first these events were blamed on some unknown, immature prankster, but then the young women began to hear the sad music of a piano echoing from a room in the basement that had been empty for years. It was well known that Roberta played the piano, though in life she preferred to play happier up-tempo tunes, and word soon spread that she had returned to the building that bore her name.

Since being identified, Roberta has moved up from being an aural presence to a visual one. Over the years Roberta's ghost has reportedly appeared in front of students. One such incident was described by a broadcasting major named Monica in an article in *The Northwest Missourian*, NWM State's campus newspaper. As Monica tells it, two female students saw a woman standing in front of a window as they walked to their car, which alone does not seem strange. But according to Monica "…with the way the beds were set up and the layout of the room, it was impossible for someone to be physically standing where this woman was."

Monica also described another incident, claiming that her friend Amy woke up one night to see "a silhouette walking to the bathroom the two bedrooms shared." The dark shadow moved closer towards the bathroom until "the toilet…flushed, and the shape disappeared as it got to the door." It doesn't seem to be a coincidence that both incidents involved room 115, which is among a handful of the dormitory's rooms that Roberta frequently visits.

Many of the students living in the haunted hall have taken to trying to ward off Roberta's spirit by using their hot-iron curlers to burn marks on their doors. They hope that the sight of fire damage, even minor, would drive her away. The tradition of marking the doors began immediately after one of Roberta's most bizarre outbursts.

Although her ghost can typically be described as benevolent but depressed and melancholy, Roberta's behavior on this night became frightening. The two young women who watched helplessly as Roberta's ghost lost control have consistently insisted that their names go unpublished, so they will be referred to as Leslie and Jean. The two co-eds shared a room together in Roberta Hall, just a few doors away from the room where Roberta was injured.

It was late at night and both were asleep, when Leslie felt someone slip into her bed and wrap an arm around her. At first she assumed that the visitor in her bed was Jean and was about to question her highly inappropriate behavior, when she opened her eyes and saw her roommate fast asleep in her own bed across the room. Leslie jumped out of her bed as quickly as she could. With her heart pounding fiercely in her chest, Leslie looked down to see who was in her bed, and was shocked to find that it was now empty. The disturbance woke Jean up, and she asked Leslie what was happening.

"N...n...nothing," Leslie stammered, not wanting to sound crazy. "I just had a bad dream."

"Well, try to keep it down," Jean muttered before she went back to sleep.

Leslie hesitantly got back under her covers and she tried to convince herself that she had merely dreamed that someone had gotten in bed with her. It took awhile for her to calm down enough to go back to sleep, but eventually she did.

Later that same night, Jean felt the body of a small woman climb into her bed and wrap her arm around her. Jean assumed that it was Leslie, still frightened from her nightmare. Not being the comforting type, Jean swore loudly and pushed the woman out of her bed. The figure fell to the floor with a loud thump. Jean immediately regretted what she had done and quickly sat up and turned on the lamp on her nightstand to see if Leslie was all right. She was stunned when she saw Leslie sitting up in her bed at the other end of the room, having just been awakened by the loud noise. They both looked down and saw the ghostly figure of Roberta Steel on their floor. Both girls were too frightened to scream and watched helplessly as Roberta's apparently solid apparition stood up and began to run around their room. Although no sound could be heard coming from its lips, it appeared to Leslie and Jean that Roberta's phantom was trying to scream. Roberta's spirit began to run faster and faster, until it finally vanished in a wisp of smoke.

Roberta Steel did not want to die. As much as she suffered, she still felt so connected to this world that she chose to forego the afterlife and remain here as a simple spirit.

Not until we ourselves face such a decision can we judge whether or not Roberta's choice was the right one to make.

King and Queen of the Prom

MOORHOOD HIGH SCHOOL, MOORHOOD, MINNESOTA

Sidney Holtz felt like a million bucks when he stepped out of his parents' house in the powder blue tuxedo he had rented for the prom. He had on his luckiest pair of shoes, which added an extra two inches to his height, and his hair was exquisitely feathered. His brown eyes beamed proudly from beneath his square plastic glasses with the cheetah design, and he couldn't wait to see what his date, Norma Reddy, looked like.

Both were seniors at Moorhead High School in the town of Moorhead, Minnesota, and both were looking forward to what they imagined would be the most magical night of their lives. They didn't know each other very well, having only gone out once before. Neither admitted it, but both had considered that trip to the movies a test to see if the other was suitable prom material. And despite their inexperience, both hoped that this second date would prove as romantic as they had dreamed.

Sidney drove up to Norma's house in his dad's Chevy at 7:15 PM on the dot, which was the exact time they had agreed to meet. He hopped out of the imposing green vehicle, walked happily to the front door and buzzed the doorbell. Almost immediately, the door swung open, exposing a large man with an equally large smile.

"Sidney! Come in!" beamed Norma's father, who looked as though he wrestled lions for a living, even though he was an accountant. He turned around and shouted towards the stairs that led out of the foyer. "Norma! Sidney's here!" His smile grew even wider and he motioned for Sidney to come inside.

Sidney stood there awkwardly, holding up the wrist corsage he had brought for Norma. He tried to think of some small talk he could share with Mr. Reddy, but his mind failed him, so he simply returned the large man's grin. It made his cheeks hurt.

Norma's mother interrupted their uncomfortable silence by bounding down the stairs with a smile that somehow managed to eclipse those of the two silent men.

"Norma will be right down, Sidney," she twinkled. "I can't wait to see the look on your faces when you see her. Have you got your camera ready, Jacob?" she asked her husband.

"I've got everything set up in the living room," he nodded happily.

"Are you ready?" shouted down a voice from above.

"Yes, honey," Mrs. Reddy called back.

From the top of the stairs, Sidney saw a ruffle of spangled white as Norma slowly made her entrance. With each step he saw more of her and by the time he got to her face it was all he could do not to shout out "yahoo!" and jump up and click his heals together. Norma had always been pretty, but after the hours she had spent preparing for this moment, she looked like she could be a movie star.

Sidney was so enthralled by the vision in front of him that it took him a moment to come up with the one phrase that best summed up what he was feeling.

"Dy-no-mite," he whispered just loud enough for everyone to hear.

The next half hour flew by as Sidney gave Norma her corsage, which matched her dress perfectly, and as they posed for photographs in the Reddys' living room. It was 7:50 PM by the time they got into Sidney's father's car and started on their way to the Moorhead High gymnasium. It was all Sidney could do to keep his eyes on the road. Norma looked so good that the temptation was to forsake their safety and just stare at her. As he fought his internal battle, Norma took out a compact from her purse and looked at herself in the mirror.

"Do you really think I look good?" she asked Sidney sincerely.

"Uh, yeah," Sidney answered incredulously, as if he had just been asked the stupidest question in the world.

"Thanks," she smiled happily.

That exchange apparently exhausted the flow of their conversation, and they drove towards the school in silence. Sidney turned on the radio to a station that featured Elton John singing with Kiki Dee. As he began to sing along, he noticed that Norma was toying with her corsage.

"Something wrong?" he asked her.

"The wrist thing is loose. I can't keep the flowers straight."

"Let me see."

Norma put her arm in front of Sidney who tried to keep one eye on the road and one eye on the corsage while he steered with one hand and fiddled with the wrist band with the other. He saw that the band had notches so it could be loosened and tightened and he tried unsuccessfully to tighten it with his free hand. Instead, he managed to loosen it and it slid off Norma's wrist and into his lap.

Instinctively, Norma grabbed at it as it fell off and accidentally hit Sidney in the one place a man never wants to get hit. Sidney grimaced and caused the car to swerve into the other lane in front of an oncoming 18-wheeler. Norma and Sidney didn't make it to the prom. It was over by the time their bodies were finally pulled from the wreckage of their collision. They were only a half block away from the high school parking lot.

The school mourned their untimely deaths, and they were posthumously named the king and queen of next year's prom. Three days before the event was to take place, the prom committee commandeered the gymnasium and set about transforming it into an underwater kingdom. The theme was "Atlantis, City Under the Sea," and various images of mer-people were intermingled with cardboard cutouts of fish and other sea life. Most of the committee members couldn't stay late, and as the sky turned dark, they began to leave, one by one. By 8:30 only three students were left. Tina, Jenny and Billy could not leave a job until it was done, and they were committed to staying until the gym looked perfect. As members of the student council, yearbook committee, debate squad and virtually every other student organization that didn't require athletic skill, the three felt as though the success of the prom had been placed squarely on their shoulders.

By 9:00 PM they had achieved that perfection and packed up their stuff, turned off the gym lights and made their way out of the school towards Billy's car, which sat alone in the parking lot. They were almost out the door, when from behind them they heard the distant sound of a peppy pop duet. As far as they knew they were the only people left in the school, so they went back inside to investigate. As they walked closer towards the music they realized that the song was "Don't Go Breaking My Heart" and that it was definitely coming from the gym.

The gym was still dark and the music was coming from the corner where they had set up the sound equipment. Jenny flipped on the lights and the three saw that the gym was exactly as they had left it. Tina walked over to the turntable that was still playing the song and turned it off. The three spent the next half hour searching because they were afraid that some pranksters intended to do harm to the decorations they had spent so much time and energy on (it had happened before). They found no one.

The next night the same three, concerned that the likely vandals had snuck out of the school before they found them, decided to watch over the gym in case the perpetrators returned. By 10:00 they were satisfied that no one was going to try anything and they left the school. This time they got all the way to Billy's car, which was parked close to the entrance, when they heard the same song again. Having been entrusted with a key to the school so they could go about their duties, they went back inside. This time they came prepared with flashlights. They crept quietly into the gym. As Tina aimed her flashlight towards the center of the gym, she caught the flash of a white dress. Silently, she got the attention of her cohorts and together they aimed their flashlights in the same direction. There, for just over a second, they saw a young couple dancing happily. The boy wore a powder blue tuxedo and the girl looked just like a movie star. But as soon as the spirits realized that they had been seen, they vanished.

Thanks to the two large pictures they had set up on the stage, they knew that the two ghosts were this year's king and queen of the prom. More than a little shocked, they somehow managed to convince themselves that what they had seen was just the result of working too hard. They were ready to dismiss the incident completely, but decided to satisfy their curiosity by staking out the gym on the last night before prom. They stayed until midnight, and after seeing and hearing nothing out of the ordinary, they decided that they had been hallucinating and started to leave. When the music started again as they reached the door, they turned and ran as fast as their feet could take them and turned on the gym's lights as quickly as they could. Once again, for just a moment, they saw the phantom king and queen.

Not sure what to do, they decided to not tell anyone what they had seen and heard and the prom went off without a hitch. It was only when Jenny got a panicked phone call a year later that the truth of what they had seen came out. The call came from the current head of the prom committee who wanted to know if Jenny, the previous holder of that position, had seen or heard anything strange before the big night. Jenny told the anxious young girl what had happened and how the ghosts only came out when they thought they were alone. She assured the girl that the phantom couple was nothing to be afraid of and that they wouldn't harm anyone or anything.

Ever since then, the former head of the prom committee has made it his or her business to inform the current head about the school's two ghosts and to assure them that they just want to have fun. They also tell whoever is in charge to make sure to keep a copy of Elton John's greatest hits wherever they set up the sound system.

2

Before They Were Schools

When a school takes over a property, it not only inherits problems with the plumbing, the pests and the foundation, but it also inherits the spirits that possessed the property before there was a school there.

A Tunnel to Nowhere

BAYLEY-ELLARD CATHOLIC HIGH SCHOOL, MADISON, NEW JERSEY

One of the many reasons school faculties are so unwilling to publicly admit that their schools are haunted is the fear that they will be inviting the curious public to trespass on school property in the hopes of catching a glimpse of some bizarre supernatural phenomenon. Most ghost hunters make sure that they have permission before exploring a building or an area, and most are willing to take no for an answer, but there is a minority who are overcome by curiosity and will do just about anything to get inside. There are whole websites devoted to photographs taken inside haunted buildings, and it isn't uncommon for the people who took them to admit that they snuck onto the property to take the photos.

The problem is one that the faculty of the Bayley-Ellard Catholic High School in Madison, New Jersey, know only too well. Founded in 1850 as the School of Our Lady of Assumption, a grammar school, it became a high school in 1920. Twenty-three years later, thanks to a $100,000 donation from a wealthy patron, the school purchased the 40-acre Walker Estate, which included a mansion, conservatory and carriage house. These buildings were remodeled into proper schoolhouses and have been in constant use ever since, with the exception of the carriage house, which, because of constant flooding in its basement, was boarded up in the mid-1980s. When the decision was made to close down the carriage house, no one at the school suspected it would cause Bayley-Ellard to be overrun by curious thrill seekers in search of the supernatural.

Many of these people are just naturally attracted to any old, boarded-up building, but the majority have come looking because of the stories attached to the carriage house ever since the school had bought the land. Some have even surmised that the official reasons for closing up the building, the flooding problem and its general decrepitude, were just a cover-up for the real reason—it's haunted.

Before the school bought the estate, it was owned by the Walkers, a wealthy family whose riches were eventually bled away by years of misfortune. Their first encounter with tragedy occurred when the original mansion burned to the ground, killing a young girl who was the daughter of one of the Walker's servants. They rebuilt the mansion, spending a great deal of money, only to find more death and misery during the attempted reconstruction of the tunnel that connected the mansion to the carriage house. Built so that the servants could more easily transport the horses to and from the mansion during the cold winter months, the tunnel had been greatly damaged by the fire. The strong wooden beams that had been used to keep the earth from collapsing had been weakened, and when a crew of carpenters went in to repair them and reconnect the mansion to the carriage house, the beams collapsed. Three men died, and it was decided that it was even too dangerous for their bodies to be recovered. That half of the tunnel was closed off. The other half of the tunnel that led out from the carriage house was still safe and it was used for storage. It didn't take long for people

to stop storing things there, when they began hearing voices and the cries of the men who were buried on the other side of the tunnel.

It was thanks to these unearthly moans that the tunnel was emptied and its large wooden door sealed shut with wooden planks and a large metal lock. No one wanted so graphic a reminder of what had happened there. It was decided that it would be best to just forget that the tunnel ever existed, which it almost was. After a series of poor investments robbed the Walkers of their remaining fortune, they were forced to sell their property. When they did, they never mentioned the half tunnel under the carriage house, nor did they mention that people could sometimes hear the tearful cries of a frightened little girl in the mansion.

In 1944, the school had been open on the Walker Estate for a just under a year when the secret of the carriage house's haunted tunnel was finally discovered. During that time the carriage house was used for a variety of classes, and the students who attended them soon began talking about the building's basement. Even though no one knew what had happened years before, the carriage house basement had already earned a reputation for being haunted. By then, the basement had already developed a tendency to flood, and as a result, it had a dank, unpleasant smell that drove away many potential explorers. But during one hot summer day, when the basement was at its driest, a group of four students decided to sneak into the building after school and find out once and for all if it really was haunted.

The four young ghost hunters, Toby, John, Robert and Joseph, had pledged to each other that no matter what they saw, they would not run. Unsure of what they might encounter, they each carried a tool that might come in handy. Using lanterns to illuminate their way, they were disappointed to find that the basement was empty and bore little sign of any ghostly inhabitants. They were about to leave when Robert noticed a large imposing lock just a few feet away. Excited, he called his friends over. It didn't take long for them to guess why the lock was there, and they all theorized about what lay on the other side. Fortunately, Joseph had a hammer, which they used to remove the wooden planks, leaving the lock as their only obstacle. As it turned out, Toby, having long been obsessed with the exploits of Harry Houdini, had spent many hours over the past year learning how to pick locks. He got down on his knees and spent a long, sweaty hour grappling with the lock before he was finally rewarded with the satisfying click.

Their hearts raced as they opened the door and stepped into the empty tunnel. As soon as they were in, they could hear the faint whisper of voices ahead. Frightened, but determined to uphold their vow not to run, they continued to move forward, the sounds growing louder and more distinct with each step. Soon they could tell what the voices were saying. They were begging the boys to come and rescue them. Their cries were so heart-felt and genuine that the four boys began to believe that they had somehow stumbled upon an accident that had just occurred. They quickened their pace and tried to fig-ure out what could have happened. They decided that the most likely scenario was that another group of curious ghost hunters had found the other entrance to the tunnel and had some sort of accident along the way.

Finally, they came to the wall of earth that marked the end of the tunnel. They could hear the voices as if the men were right beside them. Robert had brought a shovel and he began to dig at the earth to get to the men. As he shoveled, the other three boys used their hands to move the earth. They soon became so focused on their rescue attempt that they failed to notice when they were joined by three men. It wasn't until Toby turned, and saw that the man beside him was transparent, that he realized something strange was happening. He stood up and saw two more ghostly apparitions. It took a moment for him to take in the specters before he could think of what to say or do. Finally, it occurred to him that the most reasonable reaction would be to scream and run for his life, which is what he did. The other three boys looked up from their task to see what the disturbance was. Again, it took them a moment, but when they did, their vow not to run was instantly forgotten. When the reached the exit, they shut the door, locked it and resealed it with the planks. They all vowed not to tell anyone about what they had seen, but within a week everyone at the school had heard about what had happened. From then on reports of ghosts at the carriage house became commonplace. The faculty chose to ignore the stories and treated them as figments of overactive imaginations, or at least that seemed to be the official position.

Many who have explored the old carriage house since it was closed have been shocked to discover that no attempt was ever made to remove items that might still be of use. Desks, chairs, books and science equipment can to this day be found inside the building, as if the decision to close the building was made suddenly and without warning. Many who have trespassed on the site have speculated that something occurred during the 1980s that forced the school to make the carriage house off limits. What happened has never been adequately explained. However, no evidence of supernatural phenomena has ever been found by the trespassers to back up their theory.

But because three feet of water covers the basement's floor, few have ever tried to explore the legendary tunnel where the school's best-known ghost story took place. The chances of any exploration ever happening becomes less likely as the school's faculty takes more steps to discourage trespassers from touring a building they consider a safety hazard. It seems unlikely that the truth of events in the Bayley-Ellard carriage house will ever be revealed.

Carmelita

PENINSULA SCHOOL, MENLO PARK, CALIFORNIA

James Coleman loved his wife, and it isn't difficult to understand why. Carmelita was a beautiful young woman whose intelligence and quick wit were well tempered with a poise and natural kindness that made her presence always welcome wherever she went. Those who knew her described her as "sparkling" and she gleamed with the same intensity as the emeralds she so loved to wear. They were married in 1880, and as a gift to his glittering bride, James built her a mansion. James was a businessman and California assemblyman, and his wealth allowed him to build her the finest home in all of Menlo Park. But his wealth was not enough to spare him the tragedy that kept them from ever living in it.

While the mansion was being built, the couple lived in a luxurious hotel suite in San Francisco. Construction on the mansion was completed two years later in 1882, but James' business and political interests required him to travel so frequently that by 1885 they were still living in the same hotel suite. In all that time, they had never even

been able to visit the beautiful home that had awaited them for the past three years. Carmelita never once complained about their living arrangements or about James' constant traveling, and she made every effort to enjoy the time that the two did have together. Having grown up privileged, Carmelita enjoyed doing small chores for her husband; she found them uniquely liberating. All her life she had never had to lift a finger, and now she enjoyed the accomplishment that came from doing these simple tasks. In the end, it was the strange joy she took from these jobs that would make James a widower.

James had returned home from another business trip and was so exhausted that he went straight to bed. While he slept, Carmelita decided to unpack his luggage for him. Although James had never asked her to, unpacking was one of the chores she liked to do for him every time he returned. This night she found a new item inside of one of James' bags. During his trip, James had heard about a gang of thieves who were attacking wealthy-looking men in San Francisco so, as a precaution for his return, he had bought a pistol. But the trip home had been so fatiguing that all thoughts of urban gangs had vanished from his mind, and he forgot all about his new firearm. If he had remembered, he would have warned Carmelita about it, because by now he had grown accustomed to her unpacking for him, but instead he went right to bed and slept blissfully, until a shot rang out.

As Carmelita was unpacking she felt a strange new object inside one of the bags. It was cold and unfamiliar. As she lifted it out of the bag, it became clear that it was some sort of firearm. Although her father was an avid hunter and had a large collection of rifles and pistols, Carmelita had never held one before. It was heavier than she thought it would be. She ran her hands along its surface and came across the trigger. Without thinking, and purely out of curiosity, she pulled it. It had never occurred to her that it might be loaded. The bullet hit her in the stomach at almost point blank range.

As soon as he heard the sound, James knew what had happened. He rushed out of his bed and found his young wife dead on their hotel room floor. He never recovered from the shock. He never visited the empty mansion he had built for her, and he sold it as soon as he could. Over the next three decades the house was purchased by a variety of owners, who never stayed long. The house's dour and brooding atmosphere was the explanation most often given for people's unwillingness to make it their permanent residence. In 1906 it was said that the house's gloomy atmosphere proved too much for one emotionally fragile young woman who, in a fit of suicidal depression, hurled herself down its steep front steps. By the time her flailing body hit the bottom, she became just another reason to believe that someone or something didn't want people living there.

By the early 1920s the Coleman mansion had become a temporary dormitory for students attending St. Joseph's Seminary while the permanent one was being built in the nearby Los Altos Hills. When the young clerics moved out, the building seemed destined to remain empty for a long time. Finally, a group of parents, led by Josephine Duvenck, who were concerned about the overcrowded conditions of the area's public schools, decided to form their own school. The Peninsula School was founded in 1925, and the Coleman mansion seemed the perfect place to set up shop. Basing their school's philosophy on the teachings of John Dewey, the famed American intellectual, the parents decided that the school would not follow the same reward and punish curriculum of most public schools. Instead, the children would be allowed to follow

their own inclinations and learn by doing instead of by rote memorization.

In 1929 the school purchased the mansion from the local archdiocese for $26,500, which was just over one-quarter of what James Coleman had paid to build it. The kindergarten to grade eight school has remained there ever since, where it has turned out thousands of children, the most famous being 60s political folk singer Joan Baez (her family served as house parents for the students who boarded at the school). During those years the faculty and students have battled against the building's grim atmosphere. Various reconstructions over the years have helped but even now, the gothic gloom of the mansion is still discernible.

The gloom is the least of the school's worries. Just months after Carmelita Coleman died in 1885, rumors of a ghostly presence at the mansion began to spread. It didn't take long for the school faculty to discover that these rumors were well founded and a good reason why the beautiful building always seemed to have so many new owners.

The ghost of Carmelita Coleman sparkles even more than she did in life. Virtually every sighting and report of her ghost describes a thin, beautiful woman dressed in a thin nightgown—what Carmelita was wearing when she accidentally shot herself—whose whole aspect shimmers transparently in a distinct shade of emerald green. But despite the glittering nature of her apparition, the look on its face is said to be one of loss and misfortune.

Some have questioned why she would chose to haunt a building that she had never so much as stepped in during her life. But it isn't hard to imagine that during the five years she was living in that San Francisco hotel room, the dream of the mansion that sat waiting for her would be strong enough to keep her attached to it, even after her death.

Two stories involving the school's green ghost both involve a teacher named Joe Starr. Joe was alone the first time he saw the green lady. He was walking down a dark hallway when he saw a glowing figure floating at the other end. Curious, he turned on a light and was surprised to see the spectral figure of Carmelita Coleman. According to Joe, the two stood there and studied each other for several minutes before the spirit faded from sight. The second time Joe saw her was at a special school sleep-in. He and 20 students were in their pajamas and sleeping bags in a carpeted classroom, when Carmelita's ghost entered unexpectedly. It was late and Joe, a chronic insomniac, was the only one awake. The green phantom stood there and watched over the group of children for about five minutes before fading away. The next day the children talked about seeing a beautiful green see-through woman in their dreams and drew pictures of her to prove it.

Though Carmelita is the ghost most often encountered in the school's rooms and hallways, some believe that the ghost of the young woman whose inexplicable despair drove her to fling herself down the mansion's staircase is also present. Never seen, her ghost has been heard throughout the building, usually late at night. A former Peninsula School caretaker, Ken Coale, tells of this sad ghost's typical activities.

It was 3 AM, and Ken was alone in the building. He had gotten only a few hours sleep the night before, and he was exhausted. Worried that he might cause an accident if he tried to drive home, he decided to sleep on the couch in the staff lounge. He had only been asleep for a half hour when he heard the sound of loud footsteps coming from above on the second floor. Ken opened his eyes and tried to think of a single person who would have a good reason to be there that late at night. He quickly concluded that whoever was up there was probably up to no good. Hesitantly, he left the staff room and went upstairs. As he moved closer, the sounds became louder. Just as he got to the second floor, a door flew open. Ken stepped in quickly but the dark room seemed to be empty. As he moved to turn on the light, the door slammed shut behind him. Even with the light on, the room was empty. He immediately opened the door to see if he could spot anyone running away, but he saw and heard nothing in the dark, empty hallway. The only other option for escape was the room's one window, and it appeared to be shut. He tried to open it but it seemed to be stuck. With some effort he managed to get it open but he saw that there was no ledge for anyone to stand on and that it was a straight 40-foot drop to the ground below. There was no way a person could have disappeared from the room that quickly. He decided that it had to be a ghost, but since Carmelita was always a quiet spirit, everyone assumed it was the phantom of the young suicide.

As a progressive school dedicated to new ways of teaching young children and turning them into intelligent, inquisitive teenagers, the Peninsula School shows that the more widely accepted theories towards education are not as tried and true as those who promote them would suggest. The majority of its young students come away from the school with a deeper understanding of the world around them than many of their peers who attend more conventional public schools. They also come away with a greater sense of the spiritual world, having come into contact with it at such close range. The ghosts that haunt the school, although sad, have yet to do anything that would give the children a reason to fear the world of the dead. Instead, they instill in the children a belief that the world can be as interesting as their dreams, which is as important a lesson as anyone could ever teach.

The Games Children Play

GORMAN SCHOOL,
GORMAN, CALIFORNIA

During the 1940s, the Ladies Gardening Society of Gorman, California, usually held their meetings at the large home of their president and founder, Gladys Harriman. But on special occasions, such as a presentation from a guest lecturer, they would meet at the auditorium of the local school. In 1946 the group was honored with a lecture by Reginald P. Sternhagen, a Los Angeles gardener who had worked on the grounds of such famous stars as Harold Lloyd, Mary Pickford and Jack Benny. For a full two hours the group sat spellbound in the musty auditorium as the small man with the unsettling mustache regaled them with stories of his proximity to the grass and flowers of Hollywood's elite. A brief question and answer period followed the lecture, and then the group gathered for a bit of amiable chitchat over coffee and cake. It was 9:00 PM by the time the group of mostly older women began to leave. A few stayed to help Gladys tidy up, including Martha Dewitt, an elderly woman whose greatest pleasure came from cleaning up after people and complaining bitterly about it afterwards.

Eventually Martha and Gladys were the only two women left in the building. They were getting ready to leave, when Gladys decided that she needed to visit the ladies room. Martha was left alone to slip on her coat, or at least she thought she was alone. As she moved towards the school's front door, she was surprised when a pretty young girl of about 12 blocked her path. Her hair was long and honey-blonde, and her eyes were so dark they almost seemed black. The dress she wore was dirty and parts of it were ripped and torn, and in a few places, shredded.

"I wouldn't go that way if I were you," the young girl warned Martha solemnly.

"What are you doing here at this time of night?" the elderly woman snapped at the child, not happy with the impertinence with which the girl spoke.

The girl just shrugged her shoulders and stared at Martha silently.

Martha snorted derisively at the child's rudeness and pushed past her towards the front door. Outside on the sidewalk, she stepped on a small stone, lost her balance and fell to the ground with a painful thud. When Gladys made her way out of the school, she found Martha lying on the ground, moaning in agony. She was taken to the nearest hospital, where it was discovered that she had broken her hip in two places. When Gladys came to visit her a few days later, the bedridden Martha asked her if she had seen the young girl who had warned her not to exit through the front door. Gladys shook her head. The school had appeared to be completely deserted when she left it.

At the time, neither of the two women was aware that the Gorman School, a Spanish-style building covered in stucco, was already thought to be haunted. Martha wasn't the first person to encounter the strange young girl with the eerily dark eyes, and she would not be the last.

Harriet DeRoche was the daughter of David DeRoche, a poor farmer who struggled to feed his family during the Great Depression. As thousands of men, women and children flocked to California after the horrible droughts of the Dust Bowl of the southwestern U.S. had forced them to leave their homes, David's farm was proof that times were tough even in the promised land. Always an unlucky man, David considered himself blessed to at least have the comfort of a loving family. The DeRoches were poor, but they were happy, until an accident forever changed their lives.

It was a warm summer day in 1936 when Harriet and her younger brother Matthew decided to play Cowboys and Indians. A tomboy at heart, Harriet enjoyed chasing after Matthew and tying him up whenever she caught him. Often, as a prank, she would hog-tie him and walk away for a few minutes, and Matthew would begin to cry at the thought that she might leave him there all day. This time Matthew decided to show his older sister that she wasn't going to mistreat him anymore. He had gone through a growth spurt over the past month and was sure that he now had the strength to overtake his older sister. With a loud holler that approximated what he thought a genuine Indian war cry sounded like, he caught his sister and tied her up the same way she had tied him so many times before. He ignored her angry protests and left her alone in the field, deciding as he walked away that he would rescue her in about an hour. Over the years that followed the tragic accident, Matthew never forgave

himself for being so cruel, even if his actions seem justi-
fied at the time.

What the young boy did not know was that his father
had lent the family's tractor to their neighbor, Jasper,
whose own tractor was being repaired. Jasper was getting
on in years and his eyesight wasn't what it used to be, but
he still insisted on operating the heavy machinery. When
his tractor was in working condition again, he hopped
onto the DeRoches' tractor to return it to them. Getting
to their farm required him to travel across the field where
Harriet and Matthew always played. As he drove the loud,
menacing, machine he did not see the prone figure of the
young girl tied up in the field in front of him. As the tractor approached, she screamed at him to stop but he could
not hear her over the engine's roar.

They buried Harriet on the farm, and not long afterwards, they sold the land to the county who wanted to use
it for a school. Unbeknownst to the builders, the school
auditorium was constructed right over Harriet's grave.
Almost as soon as classes began, Harriet's spirit began to
appear. Since then she has been a regular presence at the
school. She tends to be a quiet ghost, but when she does
speak, it is usually in situations like the one between her
and Martha. Even then she only says what she absolutely
has to and nothing more. For those who have seen her, the
most chilling aspect of her apparition are her almost-black
eyes that stare out in such a way as to suggest that she
knows everything that is going on around her. It is this
look that keeps her ghost from being pitiable. As horrible
as her death must have been, the dark-eyed confidence
with which she stares out at the world seems to suggest

that she's gotten over it and that she doesn't hang around the school to dwell on her past, unlike so many of her ephemeral peers. Instead, she stays at the school because, for the moment, she doesn't have any other place to be.

Blood on the Floor

MADISON ELEMENTARY SCHOOL, QUINCY, ILLINOIS

Overlooking the mighty Mississippi, the small city of Quincy, Illinois, is a place where people can feel safe. With almost 20 percent of its 40,000 residents over the age of retirement, Quincy is the typical model of quiet American life. Founded in 1825 and named after President John Quincy Adams, Quincy gained the nickname of "The Gem City" thanks to the prosperity that came so easily to its population of mostly German immigrants. Over the years that prosperity has never diminished and Quincy has avoided the pitfalls that can doom any small community. Crime has never been a problem, with only seven murders taking place between 1995 and 2002, so that the effects of such barbarity are more likely to linger in the hearts of its residents. In a large city, where crime and murder can be an unfortunate part of everyday life, it is easy to ignore and forget the horrors a person might face. But in a place like Quincy, these same events can haunt people for years, even centuries. Just ask the staff and students at Madison Elementary.

As a building, Madison Elementary is a comforting place that evokes memories of the schools we attended as

children. Made of vibrant red brick, the school has an innocence that is charming in that old-fashioned way that has long gone out of style. But its innocence is deceptive. The Rockwell-esque school was built on the site of a house that was home to one of Quincy's most gruesome murders. Although the crime was committed well over 100 years ago, the school still suffers from the effects of the paranormal aftermath.

There are no records of the crime. It occurred at a time when the young city was ill prepared to deal with such a macabre incident. It is known that no one was ever arrested for the murder and that it was never solved, but the rest of the details have been sanded away by time and word of mouth. What follows is all that is known.

One night, possibly during a storm or a clear summer day, two men, possibly burglars or drifters or both, broke into the house, which is always described as large and opulent, and were confronted by the woman who lived there. Although her name has been lost, she is always described as being elderly and as being attached to her pet bulldog. Seeing the two men from the top of the stairs, the old woman screamed and the dog barked. The two scoundrels ran to her, quickly silenced the dog and dragged her screaming down the stairs. They stilled her cries by stabbing her repeatedly with their sharp knife, leaving a trail of blood on the oak floor. Having robbed her of her life, they stashed her body in the closet underneath the stairs and then robbed her of her possessions.

It was some time before the old woman was missed. Coming upon the crime scene, investigators found the most striking aspect of the crime was the trail of red that stained the oak floor. The floor looked as though it had been painted with blood. Without any relatives to inherit it, the ownership of the house fell to the city, which, understandably, had some difficulty finding a buyer. Eventually, though, a family from Chicago bought it without acually setting foot in it. They were informed of the house's history, but having lived in "The Windy City" where such incidents were far from uncommon, they saw no reason not to buy it.

When they arrived in Quincy they were delighted by the house, which was much nicer than they had expected and worth twice as much as they had paid for it. The only problem as they saw it were the red stains that trailed along the floor. They tried to wash, sand and varnish them away, but apart from completely replacing the floor, there was nothing they could do but cover them with carpets. They also avoided using the closet underneath the stairs, because it smelled of rot and decay and because the few things they did put there fell apart when they took them out.

They lived in the house for several months before they were confronted by the strange noise that came from the stairs. At random times during the day, they could hear what sounded like a dog going up and down the steps. Eventually, they found out about the murdered woman's beloved bulldog, which had also died that night.

Soon even their big city nonchalance would not allow them to ignore that, along with the blood-soaked floor, the closet of decay and the phantom pooch, the doors on the east side of the house were starting to fly open without warning, as if to suggest that they should leave. When the city offered to buy the house back so it could build a school on the property, the family happily agreed and moved back to Chicago, where violent crime may have been more frequent, but was at least less likely to invoke the supernatural.

The house was torn down and the school was built. By sheer coincidence, a broom closet was built in the same spot as the infamous closet under the stairs. It too sat empty, when it was once again discovered that anything put in it would self-destruct when it was taken out. As well, the footfalls of a heavy dog could on occasion be heard going up and down the school's stairs, and the custodian would sometimes complain about red stains that would suddenly appear on his clean floors. In 1982, the school was almost destroyed by fire. Whether the fire was a simple case of arson, a freak accident or a sign that the school's spirits wished to rid themselves of their home has never been established.

Madison Elementary is, by all accounts, a great school. Although it remains haunted by a grisly crime from the past, it is still a place where children can go and receive the best possible education that can be expected anywhere in the country. With its picturesque architecture and hardworking staff, it is a shining example of a place that refuses to allow its past to cripple its future.

The Entity

CHI OMEGA SORORITY AND
PHI DELTA THETA FRATERNITY,
TALLAHASSEE, FLORIDA

Near Tallahassee's Florida State University there are two buildings that share the same terrible burden. They are the Chi Omega sorority house and the Phi Delta Theta fraternity house. To look at them one would never guess that they figure so prominently in the case of one of America's most brutal and cunning serial killers. But in the late 70s, each house was affected by the presence of the man known as "The Deliberate Stranger," Ted Bundy. At the beginning of 1978, four young women at Chi Omega were attacked by the madman who was living in the boardinghouse that would eventually become the Phi Delta Theta house. Today both houses bear the psychic scars of his actions.

What makes the story of Ted Bundy so unique and chilling is that he could have been a great man. Handsome, charming and intelligent, he was by all appearances the very antithesis of the psychopathic killer, making him even more dangerous. He set off none of the warning signals that would tell a young woman to avoid him, and even when evidence against him began to mount up, the police were hesitant to move their investigations in his direction. Like John Wayne Gacy, Bundy did charity work and campaigned for the Republican Party, and nothing in his past suggested that he was capable of the crimes he committed. Bundy was smart enough to exploit his attributes perfectly, until finally, the evidence against him grew too great to ignore.

In November 1974, Bundy tried to kidnap a 17-year-old named Carol DaRonch in Salt Lake City, where Bundy had moved from Seattle, so he could study law. Luckily she managed to escape, but Debbie Kent wasn't as fortunate. Bundy picked her up after Carol ran away from him. She did not survive the encounter. After Bundy had been captured he confessed that he felt he had been possessed by a force he called "The Entity," which made him commit his crimes. In 1975 "The Entity" was almost stopped when a highway patrolman in Salt Lake City pulled Bundy over for driving without his lights on after dark. Patrolman Bob Haywood was immediately suspicious when he found a balaclava, a stocking mask, a pair of handcuffs and an iron bar on the floor of Bundy's car. Haywood arrested Bundy, who calmly insisted that the headgear was for skiing and that he had found the other items in the trash. Police searched Bundy's apartment and there found a brochure for Snowmass ski resort in Colorado, site of the recent murder of a young woman named Caryn Campbell. Bundy was put in a lineup and was instantly identified by Carol DaRonch, who shook as she realized how close she had come to death.

Bundy was sentenced to 15 years for kidnapping DaRonch, but before he could begin serving his term, he was sent to Colorado to be tried for the murder of Caryn Campbell. It looked like Bundy would no longer be a threat to the public. All that changed in December 1977, when he escaped from his prison cell thanks to a smuggled-in hacksaw blade. He traveled as a fugitive throughout various states until he reached Florida at the beginning of January 1978. He ended up in Tallahassee where he rented a room at a boardinghouse known as "The Oak," which was named for the huge moss-covered, 1000-year-old oak tree growing in its front yard. While in prison Bundy had become convinced that he had managed to overcome "The Entity" and that he would be able to start a new life in Florida. But the temptation that freedom brought was too powerful, and Bundy let himself be taken over by his dark side again.

On January 15, he broke into the Chi Omega sorority house and killed two students, Margaret Brown and Lisa Levy, and seriously injured two more. It wasn't until the middle of February, after he had claimed one more victim, Kimberly Leach, that he was caught driving a stolen car to Pensacola. Three months later he went on trial for the murders of Margaret and Lisa, serving as his own defense counsel. Despite the mountain of evidence against him, Bundy protested that he was innocent and some people actually believed him. Thanks to his charm and good looks, Bundy received hundreds of letters of support, most from women who often included marriage proposals. But Bundy's natural charisma was not enough to save him. He was convicted by the jury and was sentenced to die in the electric chair. Bundy spent the next ten years doing everything he could, from using legal tactics to confessing to crimes no one knew he had committed, to put off his walk down the green mile. Eventually, there was nothing else he could do, and on January 24, 1989, he was executed.

After that night in January, the Chi Omega house was never the same. The violence it saw transformed its atmosphere from delight to despair so completely that it was impossible for anyone to ignore. Even though the change in perception was more than understandable for the girls who lived there when the murders occurred, it didn't explain why it remained so for the girls who joined the sorority years later. Most of today's Chi Omega sisters weren't even born when the murders happened, yet they too admit to feeling a gloomy sensation in the house that is unlike any they have ever encountered. The feeling of melancholy is so palpable that many have concluded it must be a supernatural phenomenon. No one has ever seen the ghosts of Lisa Levy and Margaret Brown, but that does not mean their spirits are not still connected to the house in which they died. Instead of becoming full-on apparitions, they may have decided to simply remain as an uneasy feeling to remind their sisters to be wary and constantly vigilant.

Unlike the Chi Omega house, the Phi Delta Theta's link to the Bundy case is not immediately apparent, unless one recognizes the large oak tree that covers its front lawn. The Phi Deltas bought and remodeled the boardinghouse where Bundy stayed and where he once again allowed himself to be overcome by "The Entity." It was a decade after Bundy's arrest before this coincidence would have a paranormal effect on the frat house. Two weeks after Bundy was executed, two female students walked by the house and noticed a young man standing on its porch. Since he was good looking, they gave him the once over and both gasped.

"He looks just like...," they spoke together, without having to finish the sentence. Bundy's execution had been big news for the past couple of weeks, and his picture had appeared all over the media.

The girls stopped and looked at the young man, who appeared not to notice them. Knowing that the killer had once lived in the house, they wondered aloud if the young man's appearance was just a bizarre coincidence or if he had somehow been made up to look like Bundy as some sort of sick joke. As they stood and debated the possibilities, their mouths dropped open simultaneously when the young man vanished right before their eyes.

Since then no has been able to confirm or deny if Bundy really did return to "The Oak" after his death. It has been suggested that the whole thing was a prank perpetuated by the fraternity to give them a story they could use to scare young gullible coeds, but there is still the frightening possibility that Bundy's spirit remains earthbound. Even worse, there is the chance that the apparition may be "The Entity" that Bundy claimed lived inside him and forced him to kill. Thanks to Bundy's trip to the electric chair, there is the terrifying possibility that his spirit is now free to explore its every unspeakable whim—another excuse, perhaps, for people of Tallahassee to lock their doors at night.

Where Not to Build a School

CLYDE A. ERWIN HIGH SCHOOL, ASHEVILLE, NORTH CAROLINA

Clyde A. Erwin High School in the town of Asheville, North Carolina, found itself embroiled in controversy in 1998 and 1999, when the names and mascots of their sports teams were declared racially insensitive. For years the boys' and girls' teams were known as the "Warriors" and the "Squaws," and they were represented by Native American mascots in a way that caused many aboriginal people to feel uncomfortable. When the local school board was asked to do something about these offensive names and images, they decided, in a move that many saw as cowardly, that they would let the students decide. The school's principal, Malcolm Brown, strongly supported the name change and did his best to educate the students about why the names were so inappropriate. In the end, the students voted to keep the names for the sake of tradition. Their decision led the U.S. Justice Department to launch an investigation into the matter, and eventually, the school was forced to change the "Warriors" mascot into a more ethnically neutral character and drop the name "Squaws" entirely. With all the controversy going on, it would seem that the school had little time to worry about anything else, but thanks to the history of the property on which the school sits, political incorrectness was the least of its worries.

Just outside Asheville in the late 1970s there was a stretch of land designated as the Old County Home

Graveyard, where anyone too poor to pay for a funeral was buried. Scores of unmarked wooden crosses were the only proof that these people once lived. When the town decided to build a new high school, the crosses were lifted out of the ground and transported, along with the bodies under them, to a field on the other side of the road. In an

ill-conceived move, the new school was built on the site of
the old graveyard. What no one realized was that the
practice of marking the graves with crosses was a relatively modern observance. In the earliest years of the
graveyard's existence, many of the bodies were dumped
together, without coffins, two or three at a time into a
grave without any marker at all. And so it was that not all
of the graveyard's bodies were moved, and the school was
built on top of ground that still contained the dead. The
indignity of being buried in such poorly tended grave-
yards tended to spawn numerous discontented spirits. But
unceremoniously moving their remains or, worse yet,
building right over them, served to make them downright
angry. Anyone who has ever stayed up late to watch an old
low-budget horror movie on TV knows that the one thing
you never ever do is BUILD A SCHOOL ON A GRAVE-
YARD! Apparently, the people responsible for the construction of the Clyde A. Erwin High School all went to
bed before those kinds of movies came on.

From the day that classes started at Clyde A. Erwin,
everything that one would expect to happen did. The
school's janitors, just getting used to the new school, were
forced to deal with mournful whispers in the dark and the
pungent smell of decomposing flesh that settled over the
school at nightfall. They caught glimpses of human fig-
ures in their peripheral vision, but whenever they turned
to get a better look, whatever they had seen was gone.
Certain rooms in the school were always cold, no matter
what the weather was like outside. Clocks stopped working for no reason and clumps of fresh dirt were found in
places where students and faculty members never went.

When the janitors first began to talk about these bizarre incidents, they were laughed at and mocked. Since then they have refused to talk to anybody about what happens to them in the school late at night. They would rather deal with the problem themselves than be treated like fools.

One former janitor was willing to break his silence on the condition that his name went unpublished. He confirmed that he had seen and heard the phenomena mentioned above many times, but he also had a story to tell that made those stories sound like trivial Halloween pranks. Afraid that details such as the date and year would give away his identity, he insisted on only supplying the most basic account of what happened.

I was in one of the rooms, cleaning the windows, when I started to hear this cough. It was bad. I've known people with lung cancer, and they sounded like they were singing opera compared to this. It sounded as though whoever was coughing was spitting out parts of their lung. I turned around to see who could be suffering like this and no one was there, but the sound didn't stop, and it was definitely coming from the room I was in. By then I'd become used to weird stuff like this happening. So I walked away from the windows and moved towards the door, but before I could get to it, it slammed shut! There was no way for that door to be locked from the inside like that, but no matter how hard I twisted and turned that knob, I couldn't get it to open. Then the coughing gets louder, like there was more of it. Like whoever was coughing before has been joined by someone else who sounds even worse off than the first guy does. I turned around from the door, looked around and saw that I was still the only person in the room, and then the lights went out. I was right beside the switch and flicked it up and down, but nothing happened and the lights stayed out. In the darkness I could hear that the two coughers were now joined by a third, who sounded like he had no lungs left to spit out at all. I took out my lighter and lit it up, but I dropped it when I saw what was in front of me. I was right; there were three, and it looked like their faces might have once been human, but now they just looked like bad meat. Something was oozing out of their mouths. It was red, but it looked too frothy to be blood. I only saw them for a split second, but I'll never forget it. Then, like someone had pressed a button somewhere, it all stopped, and the lights went back on. I turned around, opened the door and ran like hell. Most people would have quit after that, but I stayed on for awhile because I didn't want to think of myself as a coward.

Hearing stories like this one only serves to show how trivial the school's most well-publicized controversy really was. The use of Native American mascots may have been in bad taste, but at least it was done out of ignorance. The construction of the school on a former graveyard was intentional.

3

The Sisters of the Shadows

Seriously wronged by men they loved or didn't even know, the ghosts in these stories are all members of the darkest sorority of all—the sisters of the shadows.

Peer Pressure

HENDERSON STATE UNIVERSITY, ARKADELPHIA, ARKANSAS

Of the 11,000 people who live in the city of Arkadelphia, Arkansas, a remarkable 22 percent are between ages 20 and 24. The reason for the youthful population is simple: Arkadelphia is a two-university town. It is home to both the once-Methodist and now non-secular Henderson State University and the still-Baptist Ouachita (pronounced wash'-uh-taw) Baptist University, which share the same street. They sit directly across from each other, a coincidence of locality that has understandably led to the development of a friendly rivalry between the two schools. As is often the case, students from both schools rarely socialize together, choosing instead to mingle amongst their own. Given the density of young men and women in a relatively small area, it is inevitable that, on occasion, students from Henderson and Ouachita get to know each other. This is perfectly acceptable, since Arkadelphia is not Shakespeare's Verona, where such intermingling would be met by horrible tragedy. But in the case of one young couple the allusion to the houses of Montague and Capulet is not without merit. This time the result would be one death, not two, and that death would forever affect Henderson State.

In 1910, Henderson State was known as Henderson College and was still run by Arkansas' Methodist community. The rivalry between the two schools was strong, thanks mostly to the differences in belief between

Ouachita's Baptists and Henderson's Methodists. Only a minority of students considered this theological divide of any importance, but the few that did took it very seriously. William, a handsome young man who went to Henderson, and Ruth, a gorgeous young woman who went to Ouachita, were not a part of that minority. When they saw each other for the first time at the lunch counter of the local drug store, they did not see spiritual and scholastic rivals. Instead, they each saw the most physically attractive member of the opposite sex that it had ever been their privilege to encounter. Drawn by the magnetism of their own charisma, they could not help but sit next to each other and start a conversation, which led to William's proposal that they see each other later that evening. Ruth agreed and gave him her address. At that moment, it became clear to William that he had just asked a Ouachita woman on a date, but as he looked at her, the idea of his rescinding his offer became a thought he refused to even ponder.

Later that day, it became apparent to his friends who regularly hung out in his dorm room, that William was getting ready for a date. They teased him, as all good friends must, and tried their best to learn the identity of the young coed who was to be squired that evening.

William let them have their fun, but he remained silent. The truth was that his friends, as much as he liked them, were a part of that small minority who believed that girls from Ouachita were to be avoided at all costs, which was strange, since none was particularly devout. Their aversion seemed to have more to do with a natural inclination to gang up against those who were different than it did with any minor theological differences.

Unlike William, Ruth did not have a gang of friends to tease her as she got ready. She was the kind of girl whose natural shyness made it difficult for her to talk to people, a quality which, thanks to her beauty, led most of her peers to believe that she was stuck up and unapproachable. She was lonely at Ouachita. Even her roommate seldom spoke to her. If it were not for her classes, she might go for days without speaking to a single person. That was why she was so excited when she met William. For some inexplicable reason, she felt an immediate connection to him and found herself able to come up with the words that she usually found so elusive. It also probably didn't hurt that he was the handsomest boy she had ever seen. The fact that he was from Henderson didn't even factor in her thoughts. She wasn't very religious, having only gone to Ouachita because that's where her parents had wanted her to go. She wasn't even sure what the difference between a Baptist and a Methodist was, and she certainly couldn't imagine the divide being too great to cross.

After she finished dressing she went to the dorm lobby and found him already there, looking nervous in a way that she found utterly irresistible. They exchanged greetings and complimented each other on how well they looked. Ruth couldn't help noticing the looks she got from the other girls as the handsome young man escorted her out of the dormitory. More than anything, it was those looks that cemented her opinion that she had found the man of her dreams.

That first date went without a hitch, as did the second and the third and all the rest that followed. William and Ruth were such a perfect match that strangers would actually stop them on the street and tell them so. It really seemed that they were made for each other, because they shared every possible like and dislike and dreamed the same dreams. The only thing that kept things from being ideal was the tension that was developing over Ruth's desire to meet William's friends. William was afraid of what his pals would say about his Baptist girlfriend, and Ruth was afraid that his unwillingness to let her meet them meant that he was somehow ashamed of her.

Finally, William introduced Ruth to the gang. They were all obviously impressed by her beauty and remained extremely polite in her presence, but William's worst fears were confirmed when she left.

"You can't be serious," said Stanley. "Sure she's as pretty as all get out, but what would your parents say? What would her parents say?"

"Stanley's right," agreed Kenneth. George and Frank nodded.

William did his best to argue with them but the longer they talked about it, the easier it was for him to see their point of view. Yes, he loved Ruth, but was love enough? For the rest of the week he avoided her, as he tried to make up his mind about what to do. He found himself walking a lot, hoping for some sort of epiphany. One day he walked for so long he had no choice but to sit and rest. He found a park bench and flopped down on it. On the other side sat someone he recognized.

"Hi, Gertrude," he greeted her with a sigh.

"Hi, William," she replied with her usual vaguely embarrassed whisper.

William was prepared to let the conversation end there, but he noticed that Gertrude looked different than she usually did. She looked better. A lot better.

"Did you get a new hairdo?" he asked.

She nodded with a slight look of misapprehension on her face.

"It suits you," he told her.

For the first time since she had arrived in Arkadelphia, Gertrude's face broke out into a wide smile.

"Really? Do you think so?"

"I sure do."

"Thank you," she blushed. "I wasn't sure about it."

The combination of her new hairstyle, huge smile and flushed cheeks, caused William to see for the first time something that had never occurred to him as being possible. Gertrude was a knockout. That simple truth compelled him to continue their conversation. It soon became evident as they spoke that the shy girl had long harbored a crush on William. Just a half hour ago he would have been horrified at the prospect, but now it made him feel 10 feet tall. As they talked, the subject of next week's homecoming dance came up. William had been so preoccupied with his thoughts of Ruth that he had forgotten all about that important event.

"Who are you taking?" Gertrude asked innocently, assuming that some lucky girl would have already snatched up a boy as handsome and as popular as William.

A faraway look took hold of William's face. At that moment he decided that his friends were right. A relationship with Ruth would inevitably become too complicated.

This sudden mental clarity energized him, and he turned towards Gertrude and smiled.

"You. If you want to go with me, that is."

Somehow Gertrude was able to hold back her tears, but it was a hard-fought battle.

"Of course, I do," she beamed back at him, and she hoped that he wouldn't notice her hands shaking.

"That's great."

Meanwhile, Ruth didn't understand what was happening. She hadn't seen William in a week, and she couldn't understand why. It seemed like he was avoiding her. She thought back to the last time she saw him, when she met his friends, and tried to come up with an explanation for his sudden disappearance. His friends seemed to have liked her, and she couldn't remember saying or doing anything to embarrass him. Maybe she had done something without knowing about it. It wasn't considered lady-like back then for a woman to pursue a man, so Ruth fought the temptation to go to his dorm and ask him what was wrong. Just as she was about to succumb to despair, she remembered that Henderson's homecoming dance was approaching, and she convinced herself that William had vanished because he was too busy preparing for what she imagined would be their greatest date yet. If he was going all out, she decided, then so would she. She set about buying the nicest dress she could find.

She went down to the nearby general store, a small building that somehow managed to stock everything a person could conceivably want to buy. They had only a small selection of the type of dresses she had in mind, but one was perfect. As she lifted it up, she noticed another girl looking through the dresses.

"Homecoming?" she asked the girl.

The girl nodded and spoke excitedly.

"I never thought I was going to get to go, but just an hour ago the handsomest boy in the world asked me to be his date."

Ruth smiled indulgently and kept herself from saying that the girl would have to settle for being the escort of the second handsomest boy. Instead, she politely asked the girl the name of her new beau.

"William Anderson," the girl sighed.

Ruth stared at the girl.

"What is it?" The girl asked, assuming she had a spot of dirt on her face.

"Did you say William Anderson?" Ruth managed.

"That's right. Do you know him?"

A sudden rush of nausea came over Ruth, and she somehow stopped herself from fainting. Her hands began to shake; all of the blood drained from her face.

"Is something wrong?" the girl asked worriedly.

Ruth shook her head. She looked at the dress she was holding and realized that she now had no use for it. She handed it to the puzzled girl.

"Here, take this," she said. "It's the best one here."

With that, she left the store and dissolved into tears as soon as the sun hit her face. She cried all the way home, trying to think of some way that she could have been responsible for this betrayal. When she reached her room, she had concluded that she had done nothing wrong, which meant that someone else was responsible. She could not bring herself to blame William, which left only the girl in the general store. For the first time in Ruth's life she felt hate, and she didn't even know the girl's name.

As the days passed, Ruth only felt worse. It had gotten around her dorm that she had been dumped. She could hear the other girls giggle and make fun of her behind her back. By the night of the Henderson homecoming dance, she was inconsolable. She could no longer think rationally and became convinced that her life was no longer worth living. As if preparing for her own funeral, she put on the black dress she had worn when her grandmother had died. She stoically walked towards the Ouachita River, which sat at the eastern boundary of the school. After a brief moment of hesitation, she jumped in, and her body was found the next day.

News about her suicide traveled around both campuses. William's friends tried their best to convince him that it wasn't his fault, and for a brief time he almost believed them. Then he began having nightmares and hearing and seeing things when he was awake. In his dreams he saw Ruth, dressed in black, looking as she did after a night spent in the river. She would always tell him that she didn't blame him just before she crumbled into dust. When he was awake he swore he could hear her crying outside his window, and there were times when he saw a woman in a black dress briefly in his peripheral vision. Everyone assumed that he was having a guilt-induced nervous breakdown, but then his friends began to hear and see the same things.

They all managed to graduate, despite the mental toll these strange occurrences took on their psyches. When they left, it was assumed that the bizarre phenomenon would cease, but it didn't. It just moved to another building.

Female students at Henderson were soon talking about the weird things that were happening in their dormitory. They too could hear the sound of a woman crying and almost subliminally see a woman in a black dress in their peripheral vision. But not long after Gertrude graduated, the apparent ghost became a more vocal and visible presence in the dorm. Late at night the young women could hear and often see the angry ghost walking up and down the halls in search of the girl whom she blamed for stealing her true love's affections. Not knowing the girl's name, all Ruth's spirit had to go by was the dress that she gave her; the dress that Gertrude did indeed wear to the homecoming dance. It wasn't uncommon in the dorm for a resident to find that her drawers and closet had been searched, with items thrown about and disheveled. Although Ruth's ghost appears all year-round, she most frequently appears during the week of Henderson's homecoming dance. It is during the week of the anniversary of her suicide that Ruth most desperately searches for Gertrude, who has long since passed on as well.

Known now as "The Black Lady" for the dress that she wears, it is clear that Ruth's ghost is an unfortunate spirit whose obsession keeps her from ever finding peace. Perhaps as punishment for her taking that most drastic of steps, she has been given the never-ending task of finding what can never be found. Henderson State has also been punished. Although it was only the intolerance of a small minority of students that caused Ruth to take her own life, the majority, including William, did little to fight their friends' prejudices. And so the school has had to forever deal with the melancholy anger of Ruth's tragic spirit. This story reminds us that discrimination for even the most trivial of reasons can have effects that can reach beyond any mortal lifetime.

Acceptance

SAN MANUEL HIGH SCHOOL, SAN MANUEL, ARIZONA

Maria (not her real name, as per her family's wishes) never saw it coming. It all happened so fast that one second she was alive, laughing and talking to her friends, and the next she was dead on the ground, while everyone screamed and tried to figure out what had just happened. It was 1958, and they were all standing in the parking lot of San Manuel High School in San Manuel, Arizona. When the panic ended, it became clear that someone somewhere had shot Maria.

A mining town, San Manuel was only 14 years old when this tragic accident occurred. Over those years the town had grown as Mexican immigrants looking for work flocked to the new city, Maria's family among them. Maria was the youngest child in a family of eight. Her father worked in the mine and her mother took in laundry to make ends meet. Maria was a happy girl; naturally shy, she was attractive enough that other people made the effort to get to know her. She was popular at San Manuel and spent most of her time with a boy named Diego, although she didn't call him her boyfriend because her father wouldn't have approved. She was famous for her smile, which was warm and infectious. Most people found it difficult to be miserable when she was around.

On the day of the shooting she was excited because her father had finally decided that she was old enough to go to a school dance. Although she wasn't allowed to go with a boy and had to be chaperoned by one of her older brothers, it was still a major achievement given how strict and old fashioned her father was. School had just ended for the day. She and Diego and a group of their friends were talking about what they were planning to wear to the dance and what kind of music the band was going to play. Someone made a joke, and Maria giggled along with everyone else when a loud bang, like the sound of a car backfiring, erupted across the parking lot. Everyone turned to see where it had come from, but couldn't find the source. When they turned back, they began to scream and cry when they saw Maria lying on the ground in a bloody heap. It had all happened so quickly that Maria's face still bore the smile she was wearing when the shot rang out.

A group of boys ran to where the sound had come from and found a student in a car whose face was pale with panic and fear and whose hands held a small hunting rifle.

"I didn't know it was loaded," the boy wept.

Maria's death was ruled an accident, and at her funeral, Diego and the rest of Maria's friends all spoke to the guilt-stricken young man responsible and forgave him. Although their forgiveness allowed them to get on with their lives and allowed the boy responsible to get on with his, it had little effect on what this senseless moment of violence did to Maria's spirit.

One reason many people who die in accidents come back to the place where they were killed is because they had no time to accept the inevitability of their fate. Those people who deal with the sick and dying know that there are five stages a person goes through as they come to terms with their own mortality. These stages are anger, bargaining, denial, depression and acceptance. Of these stages it is the last that is the most important. Often in cases of terminally ill patients, it is only their unwillingness to accept their fate that keeps them alive. People have lived for days in agony, surviving on will alone, only to finally expire when they realize that it is simply their time to go. But when people die like Maria do, suddenly and without warning, they are robbed of the peace that comes from the final stage before dying. They've never accepted their passing so they force their spirits to return to the spot where they died.

Strange things began happening at San Manuel High just days after the shooting, but it would be months before people would ascribe them to supernatural forces, and it would be months after that before Maria was judged to be the only likely culprit. Lockers and doors could be heard slamming throughout the building. Toilets flushed all by themselves, and the showers in the girls' locker room began to spray water randomly and without warning. These were all signs that Maria had yet to realize she was dead and was desperately trying to get people to notice her. But it was only when cars that were parked on the spot where she died had trouble starting that people began to believe that she was responsible for the events. And it was then that people began to see her.

Those who have glimpsed Maria's spirit all describe it as looking sad and abandoned. Loss and confusion flicker in her eyes, and her famous smile is nowhere to be found. The friendly and pretty young girl has grown into a sad, lonely young ghost. As her spirit walks through the school halls she wonders why people ignore her and have stopped talking to her. Even as the years pass, she seems to have yet to accept that she is dead. The cleaning staff have repeatedly found unexplained messes in classrooms and hallways, as well as heard the sounds of someone crying in the halls. There have been attempts to get Maria's ghost to understand what happened to her, but so far they have all proven unsuccessful. Sadly, there is a good chance that her spirit will never accept her fate and will remain at the Arizona school for as long as it stands.

The Rebel in Her Room

STEPHENS COLLEGE, COLUMBIA, MISSOURI

In 1833, a group of men in the frontier town of Columbia, Missouri, led by a colonel named Richard Gentry, decided that their daughters had as much right to an education as their sons did. Having come to their decision, the 14 men were forced to deal with one important fact—there was no school dedicated to educating young women in the entire state. The solution was obvious; they would create their own. The Columbia Female Academy opened its doors a few months after that momentous decision. Its first incarnation was a humble affair, housed inside a Presbyterian church, where 25 young women were taught the fundamentals of English grammar, moral philosophy, algebra and celestial geography.

Twenty-three years later, in 1856, a businessman named David H. Hickman decided that the small school in the church deserved to become a larger and more prominent institution. Under his guidance the school moved into a new and larger building and became the Columbia Female Baptist Academy, a full-scale college with a much more diversified program. In the 1860s, philanthropist James L. Stephens donated $20,000 to the college and was rewarded for his generosity when the school was renamed the Stephens Female College. Since then the school has simply become known as Stephens College, and over the 170 years it has existed, has established itself as one of the best institutions dedicated to the education of women, changing with the times to teach its students to become important and productive members of society.

Over the last few decades programs have been established that allow men to attend the school in either undergraduate or graduate capacities, but there was a long period of time when, save for faculty members, it was rare to catch sight of a male on campus. The absence of a male population was a great relief to many families who sent their daughters to the school from all around the country. The last thing they wanted to be worried about was that their female offspring might be tempted to bring shame and ruination to her family's good name for the love of some rugged, illiterate Missouri cowboy. This depravation, however, often had the negative effect of inflaming desires in the students for the rare man they did encounter. Thus, a deliveryman, who in any other situation would find himself ignored by these young women from well-respected families, would be greeted by a veritable horde of blushing admirers.

In 1862, the situation was even worse than usual, since many of the male faculty members had left to take part in the Civil War. Although Missouri allowed its citizens to own slaves, it refused to join in the war and operated as a border territory with an admittedly strong Confederate bias, which meant that troops of both armies were unwelcome. Missouri's Confederate sympathies didn't stop Union troops, under the command of General Henry Halleck, from going in and taking control of Columbia, to the dismay of its citizens. Of all those opposed to the Union takeover of their town, none was more upset than the president of the Columbia Female Baptist Academy,

Dr. Hubert Williams. The thought of all those violent men congregating right next to the young women under his charge did not inspire his optimism. He saw pain and misery as the only possible result, and he was right.

Sarah June Wheeler was a natural romantic and it pained her to be kept away from the young men who were naturally attracted to her blonde good looks. She felt imprisoned at the school. Her stubborn father had forced her to attend, insisting that a young lady of her stature required a decent education. As a result, she was a poor student and made little effort to socialize with her class-mates, who regarded her as an irritating snob. The only friend she made during her time at the school was her roommate Margaret Baker, a sturdy Southern girl from Arkansas who shared Sarah's rebellious attitude. Both were very excited about the soldiers' takeover of the city, although Margaret feigned apathy because of her allegiance to the Confederacy. For several weeks they stayed up late each night giggling about how exciting it would be to meet a soldier, although they both knew that, as long as Dr. Williams had his way, they never would.

It was a Tuesday when Sarah's and Margaret's wish unexpectedly came true, although neither would have been able to dream up the circumstances under which it occurred. Sarah had barely walked two steps into their dorm room after her last class of the day when someone grabbed her from behind. The intruder clapped his hand over her mouth before she could scream.

"Hush," he whispered. "I ain't gonna hurt you." His voice was hoarse and tired and very definitely Southern. "I'm hurt bad, and I just need a place to rest. You can scream if you want, but all you're going to do is doom a man who's close to death already."

Sarah turned and saw a handsome young man dressed in the gray uniform of the Confederate forces. A blood-soaked rag was tied around his leg, covering a wound that was only a few hours old.

"Lay down," Sarah ordered.

The young man hobbled to the bed closest to him, which was Sarah's, and collapsed on it, too weak and exhausted to stand for a moment longer. Just then the door swung open, and Margaret walked in. This time it was Sarah who grabbed the surprised girl and threw a hand over her mouth.

"We've got to help him," she whispered into Margaret's ear.

Margaret looked at the wounded soldier on her room-mate's bed and figured out what was going on. She nodded that she understood, and Sarah let her go.

The two young women tended the soldier's wound as best as they could, while he told them his story. His name was Isaac Johnson, and he was a corporal in the Confederate army from Mississippi. He had been captured at the Battle of Pea Ridge and had been sent to a prison camp in Illinois, but he had managed to escape. When he finally reached a Confederate outpost, he was horrified to discover that his father was listed as one of the casualties in the attack on Nashville. It was then that he was offered, and decided to accept, a mission from which he could exact a small sliver of revenge. He would go to Columbia, Missouri, to assassinate General Henry Halleck. But his mission was thwarted when he was shot while trying to steal a Union uniform from a dead soldier. Somehow he managed to make it to the school where he climbed into the first window he found, which, by a strange twist of serendipity, opened into the one room where he was almost guaranteed asylum.

As hard as they tried, both Sarah and Margaret knew that they weren't equipped to deal with Isaac's injury. They had to bring in someone who could be of more help, but whom they could also trust not to say anything. Luckily for them, they knew exactly who to get.

Ruby was a slave, once owned by Margaret's father; he had given her to the school as a part of Margaret's tuition. She worked in the school kitchen and did other household chores. Having grown up with her, Margaret knew that Ruby was as good as any doctor when it came to taking care of people, so she ordered the elderly slave to come to their room. Ruby was shocked to see a young man lying on one of the girls' beds, but she knew enough to keep quiet and just tend to his wounds. When she was finished, Margaret instructed her not to speak of the soldier's existence to anyone and to visit him three times a day with fresh bandages and warm food. Ruby silently nodded, fully aware that no good could come of the situation.

For the next week the girls shared their room with the wounded soldier who was deeply moved by their kindness and generosity. He was especially taken with Sarah, whose beauty was a sweet antidote to the horrors he had witnessed in the battles he had fought. Sarah returned his affections, moved both by his plight and his handsome good looks. Quickly, their mutual affection grew. By the time the weekend came, both had admitted to being in love with the other. Unfortunately, Ruby had been unable to keep her secret and had whispered it to another slave who worked in the kitchen. By Monday, the whole school was abuzz with the rumor that Sarah and Margaret were hiding a Rebel soldier in their room. Upon hearing the strange piece of gossip, Dr. Williams took it upon himself to confirm its veracity. When he got to the room he found only Margaret, who insisted that she had no idea where Sarah was.

Despite Ruby's efforts, Isaac's leg had become infected and was becoming gangrenous, slowing the pair down as they made their way through the fields that dark Sunday night. As much as the pain jolted through his body, he refused to let it stop him from making his escape. He knew that a group of Confederate soldiers was encamped just a few miles on the other side of the Missouri River and that, if they could make it across, then their safety would be assured. He also knew that once he got to the camp, it would be medically necessary for the surgeon to amputate his leg. He tried not to think about that. Sarah was visibly thrilled to be a part of the adventure and appeared to be unaware of the danger. They traveled throughout the night, and just as the sun began to rise, they reached the river that they saw as their salvation.

The waters of the Missouri River ran high at that time of the year because of the heavy rains that had fallen throughout most of the month. It was a powerful river, and as soon as Sarah and Isaac stepped into it and felt its icy grip, they knew that there was a good chance they wouldn't make it across.

They didn't. The young lovers were never seen again, their bodies swept away by the force of the river.

From the moment of their deaths, the school was visited by a series of strange ghostly disturbances, especially inside the hall in which Sarah lived. The building took on a strange unearthly atmosphere that defied any conventional explanation. Some students reported seeing ghostly apparitions of former students in period dress, and others have described phantoms that closely resemble Sarah and Isaac. The school's policy towards these incidents is interestingly contradictory. On the one hand it annually treats visitors and alumni to a play about the tragic lovers, at the same time firmly denying that the school is haunted. Despite their denials, many of the students who live in the hall have no choice but to believe that something, even if not the ghosts of the ill-fated couple, haunts the hall. As much as their rational minds tell them otherwise, their senses cannot be ignored.

The Pool

For the second time in a couple of weeks an unnatural coldness took hold of Ms. Burns' Language Arts classroom at Stivers Middle School in Dayton, Ohio. The first time it happened, Charlie, the school custodian, couldn't figure out what was wrong. Somehow the room managed to feel even colder than the temperature outside. His only solution was to bring in space heaters. Fortunately, these warmed the room enough so that it was tolerable, and Ms. Burns was able continue with her classes.

Her last class of the day was 8D, and while the students sat reading a passage she had assigned to them, she started to write a paragraph from it on the blackboard. As she wrote, she heard a loud slam at the back of the classroom.

"What was that?" she turned quickly towards her students. They all looked as caught off guard as she was.

SLAM!

"If someone's…"

SLAM!

"I'm serious…"

SLAM!

Everyone turned in the direction of the noise, which seemed to be coming from beneath the floor.

"Ms. Burns, look." Geoffrey pointed towards the metal trapdoor in the floor at the back of the room. They heard another slam, and the trapdoor shook visibly.

Ms. Burns walked towards the trapdoor, enlisting help from two students along the way.

SLAM!

SLAM!

SLAM!

With her two helpers Ms. Burns lifted the trapdoor and all at once the slamming ceased and the classroom's television turned on, blaring loud static.

"SSSSSSSSSSSSSSSSSSSSSSSSSSSSSSSSSSSSSSSSSSSSSSS!"

"Turn that off," Ms. Burns ordered, as she looked into the darkness below. "Hello?" she shouted into the void, her voice echoing. "Is anyone down there?"

No response. The television had been turned off, and the room was now deathly silent as Ms. Burns and the students waited for something to happen. Nothing did. They closed the trapdoor, and with all of the students too shaken to continue, Ms. Burns dismissed everyone. She walked dazedly to Principal Argento's office and told him what had just happened. A look of concern came over his face, and he asked her if she was feeling all right and if anything stressful was happening at home. She insisted that she was perfectly okay and that her students could back up her story. Not knowing what else to do, Principal Argento shrugged and told her that he would see what he could do.

That next morning, she opened up her room's closet to put away her coat and was surprised to find that the closet light was on. She knew that it had been off when she'd left the day before.

She turned the light off, closed the door and went to her desk to finish up some marking. She opened one of her desk drawers in search of a red pen, knowing that at least a dozen should have been there.

She couldn't find one. Not amused, she emptied the drawer and sifted through its contents item by item. There wasn't a single red pen to be found. She looked through the other drawers, and they proved to be entirely free of red pens as well.

Ms. Burns sat at her desk and wondered who in the world would go through her desk and steal all of her red pens. Before she could contemplate the matter further, the first morning bell rang and the students in her home-room class began to arrive.

"Is it true?" a student asked her.

"Is what true?"

"Some kids from 8D are saying the classroom is haunted. They said that there were loud noises coming from the trapdoor in the back. Is there a ghost in here?"

"Yes and no," Ms. Burns answered quickly. "There were some strange noises yesterday, but we don't know what caused them. My guess is that an animal somehow managed to get into the space underneath the room and was banging against the trapdoor to get out." As soon as the words left her mouth, she knew how unconvincing she sounded, but she carried on anyway. "There is no ghost."

"SSSSSSSSSSSSSSSSSSSSSSSSSSSSSSSSSSSSSSSSSSSS!" The television blared out from behind her, causing her to start violently. Her heart pounded fiercely as she walked over to it and turned it off.

"There is no ghost," she repeated. "Now, open your books to chapter five."

As the day proceeded, Ms. Burns was forced to turn on the space heaters because the room once again grew abnormally frigid. She tried her best to get through the lesson plan for her classes, but all of her students were too curious about the stories they were hearing in the hallway to pay attention. Finally, the students of 8D began to arrive for the last class of the day. They murmured excitedly to each other about whether or not they would get a repeat of what happened the day before. Just as Ms. Burns was about to threaten a half-hour class detention, they all grew suddenly silent.

Shocked by their instant transformation she turned to see what caused it. There in the doorway was Mr. Argento.

"Can I see you for a moment, Ms. Burns?"

"Of course," she answered before turning back to her class. "Read quietly while I'm gone," she instructed before leaving the room and closing the door behind her.

"I talked to some people—," Mr. Argento told her before being interrupted by a loud noise from inside the classroom.

Ms. Burns turned immediately and opened the door.

SLAM!

"It's happening again!" shouted Geoffrey, pointing at the trapdoor.

SLAM!

SLAM!

SLAM!

Ms. Burns and Mr. Argento ran to the trapdoor and threw it open, exposing the blackness beneath it. They both poked their heads into it and saw nothing except a dusty tile floor on which sat a pile of cylindrical objects.

"What are those?" Mr. Argento squinted at them.

"They're red pens," answered Ms. Burns.

Mr. Argento sat down on a chair in the corner while Ms. Burns dismissed the class early for the second day in a row. When the students were gone, the two began to talk.

"I know," he admitted, before she could remind him that she had told him so.

"Well?"

"Like I said, I talked to some people," he sighed. "I think I may know what's going on, although I'm not sure I believe it."

"At this point, I'll believe anything," she admitted.

"Good," he paused as he tried to figure out the best place to start. "Do you know why there is a trapdoor in this room?"

"No."

"When they first built the school, the whole lower level of the building was the gymnasium, but in the 30s they decided they needed more classrooms and renovated everything. One of the things that needed to be taken care of was the school's indoor pool, but instead of filling it in, they decided it was cheaper to just build a room over top of it. They made the trapdoor in case we ever needed storage, which we never have."

"What does it have to do with—?"

"I'm getting to that. The pool had a history. About 10 years before they renovated, one of the school's teachers was found floating in it."

"Dead?"

"Very dead. Apparently, she was in the habit of going for a swim every Friday. They found her on a Monday. She had been in there for the entire weekend."

"So it was an accident."

"No," Mr. Argento shook his head. "When they found her she wasn't wearing her swimsuit. She was in her street clothes, and that wasn't all. In one hand, she held a pointer, which was broken in half, and in the other she held a locket. When they opened it they found a picture of her parents and a picture of man, but they couldn't tell who it was because his head had been ripped off."

"So who did it?"

"They never found out, but there was a chief suspect. It turned out that Miss Keller—that was her name—was a beautiful woman who was popular with her male students. They all did everything they could to impress her, but there was one student, a senior named Jerome, who was obsessed with her. He spent every second he could with her and went out of his way to help her. There was a rumor, never substantiated, that the two were lovers. When her body was found, everyone assumed that he had killed her in a jealous rage."

"Why wasn't he arrested?"

"Because they never found him. The last time anyone saw him alive was on the Friday that she was killed. Most people assumed that he had run away and changed his identity, but some believed that he was killed by the same person who killed Miss Keller—the man whose photograph she kept in her locket."

"So who is the ghost?"

They sat together for another hour trying to think of ways to deal with their unique problem.

"Do you know anybody who can deal with this?" Ms. Burns asked.

He shook his head.

The next day, Ms. Burns hesitated before entering her classroom. She felt helpless. As a teacher she was used to being in control, and a part of that meant always knowing what was going on. Now, she didn't. She had no idea. She walked inside and did her best to follow her normal routine. She put away her coat—the closet light was off as it should have been—and sat down to do some work—nothing was missing from her desk. The first bell rang, the students came in and everything seemed normal. Her students were still excited about the events, but she managed to subdue them enough to get some work done. The room stayed warm, and the television stayed off. She felt as if someone, or something, was toying with her. As the last class of the day began, a knot of anxiety twisted in her stomach as she waited for the inevitable. Much to the chagrin of the students of 8D, who had grown used to getting out of class early, the inevitable never came. There wasn't a single sign of the ghost. For the next three months the classroom remained completely normal. Eventually, both she and her students managed to put the strange incidents into the back of their minds, where they were not forgotten, just put on hold. Finally, Ms. Burns concluded that her classroom was safe again.

"SSSSSSSSSSSSSSSSSSSSSSSSSSSSSSSSSSSSSSSSSSSSS!"

Ms. Burns jumped and turned towards the television set. The screen was filled with the white chaos of static. But when she looked more closely, she could see a figure reflected in it.

Ms. Burns turned around slowly. She dropped the book she was holding. She didn't scream, but her students did.

Hovering above the trapdoor was the figure of a beautiful woman with long white hair. In one hand the ghost held a broken pointer, and in the other it held a locket. It opened its mouth to speak, but all that came out was a mouthful of water.

Ms. Burns stood frozen to the spot. Her brain raced to come up with something to say or do, but nothing seemed appropriate. Finally, she spoke without thinking about what she was saying.

"Miss Keller, I'm sorry about what happened to you," she managed to keep her voice calm and sincere. "I don't know why you're here, but if there is anything we can do to help, please do something to let us know. Until then, I have to ask you to leave. You're disturbing my class, and we have work to do."

Ms. Burns had no idea if the specter understood her or what it would do, so she prayed silently that she would have the strength and intelligence to deal with whatever happened.

The ghost of Miss Keller stared at her until tears began to fall from its eyes. The TV set turned itself off, and a strange pitying calm came over the students. The ghost tried to speak once again but still could not. Water dribbled out of its mouth, drowning out its words, but somehow everyone was able to understand what it said, and they accepted its apology. Slowly, the ghost floated down into the trapdoor until it disappeared from sight. For the first time in three months, 8D got to leave class early.

After that, things did not return to normal. On occasion, the classroom would become cold, and the closet light would be on when it shouldn't have been. Objects would still go missing from her desk, but they were always found in the same spot under the trapdoor, and Ms. Burns got so used to the television suddenly turning itself on that she didn't even notice when it did. The ghost of Miss Keller never reappeared, but her presence was still felt, except that now there was no fear, only pity.

Word spread about the ghost, and almost every student who went to Stivers that year claimed to have been in the class that saw it. Psychics and journalists came from all over to study the case and to write about it, and many came away with varying versions of events, but one thing always stayed the same. In each case, Ms. Burns was always described as an excellent teacher.

Thumbing a Ride

UNIVERSITY OF BRITISH COLUMBIA,
VANCOUVER, BRITISH COLUMBIA

With two words, a young woman named Donna Grainger forever sealed her fate. They were simple words that she had said a thousand times before, usually when talking to her boyfriend Oliver. They came out of her mouth so naturally, that she often wasn't aware she had even spoken them, but every time she did, Oliver would slowly count to 10 and try to remember why he loved her.

"Shut up," were the two words that left Donna standing alone on 16th Avenue West in Vancouver, on the campus of the University of British Columbia.

Donna and Oliver, both students at the university, were driving in his Volkswagen to Donna's apartment after a late night studying in a mutual friend's dorm room. Over the course of the evening, the couple and their friends took a break from their books so they could partake in some of the experimental activities the late 60s were famous for. Neither was clearheaded as Oliver drove Donna home, and during the drive, they started an argument that would have confounded even the most focused observer. Both became enraged with the other as they argued, even though neither was making any sense. Finally, Donna said the two words she always said when they argued, and Oliver slammed his foot on the brake pedal and ordered her out of his car.

Donna stared at him as if she couldn't believe what he was saying.

"Get out!" Oliver repeated, his knuckles turning white as he gripped the steering wheel.

"But it's raining," Donna protested, "and the buses have stopped running."

"Not my problem," Oliver muttered. "Get out."

"Oh, quit being an asshole and take me home!" she ordered. Then she smiled seductively at him and said, "I'll make it worth your while."

Oliver turned to look at her. Usually an offer like that would have been more than enough to calm him down, as Donna was a beautiful young woman, but as he stared at her blue eyes and long, straight, honey-brown hair, he only saw someone who was always putting him down. He fought the urge to give in but stood his ground. Calmly and coldly he spoke to her for the last time.

"I said, get out."

A flurry of harsh, well-chosen curses flew from her lips as she grabbed her books and opened the passenger side door and stepped out into the rain. It was coming down hard, and by the time Oliver had sped away, she was already drenched. As situations go, Donna had not experienced any as bleak. Her apartment was 20 miles away, she had no money for a cab, the buses had stopped running and she didn't know anyone on the campus well enough to ask for a place to crash. As she saw it, she only had one option. She stood on the street corner, lifted her arm up and extended her thumb to the sky, hoping that someone would see her and give her a ride home.

The hard Vancouver rain did not let up as a long and wet hour passed. In that time only a few vehicles had driven past and they had all driven past her like she wasn't even there. Her long hair was matted to her face, her body shivered and her teeth chattered. She could already feel a cold coming on. She thought about finding a dry place to wait until morning, but she remembered that the essay she needed to hand in the next day was still at her apartment, and if she left it there, she would fail a class she needed to graduate. It was an early class, so she didn't even have the option of waiting till the buses started again. By the time she got home and back to school, it would be too late.

She howled in frustration as another car drove past her, and she started to cry.

Just a mile away, a truck driver named Jimmy Stilson was fighting to stay awake after his 36th straight hour on the road. Coffee and pills weren't working anymore. He couldn't stop. He had been late with his last three runs and had been told he would be fired if it happened again.

In the distance, Donna could see the lights of Jimmy's truck speeding towards her. She tried earnestly to get his attention, but she didn't want to give the driver any unpleasant ideas.

Jimmy didn't see Donna. He was asleep. As his eyes closed, his body slumped towards his door, and the steering wheel turned with it.

The truck looked like it was going to stop right beside Donna. She clapped gratefully, until she noticed that it was coming straight for her and wasn't stopping. She tried to run, but it was too late. The 18-wheeler slammed into her, throwing her body into the air. The impact shocked Jimmy awake, and he was able to turn the truck before it hit anything else. He stopped and got out. To his horror, he found the dead body of a woman.

Oliver never forgave himself for leaving her that night. He broke down at Donna's funeral and had to be helped by his friends. He left UBC soon afterwards, and no one ever heard from him again. Jimmy was charged with vehicular manslaughter and reckless endangerment and was sent to jail, where he died of a heart attack two years into his sentence. Donna never did get that essay handed in, and that must have disturbed her spirit, because for the next 30 years her ghost has been spotted on the street where she was killed, thumb in the air, waiting for a ride.

Vancouver police, the RCMP and UBC campus security have reported her presence on 16th Avenue West. Appearing only on nights when it rains, her spirit is always described as bedraggled and forlorn. Her skin is pale and sickly white, and her eyes are sunken and empty of life. Whenever anyone has gotten out of their car to approach her, she has vanished right before their eyes.

According to one former student, who wished to be referred to only as Glen, her ghost has actually interacted with people. It isn't uncommon for students and other passing motorists to see her and stop to offer her a ride. In these cases, she will walk to the car and look inside, and if someone is sitting in the passenger seat she'll just shake her head and walk away. If, on the other hand, the passenger seat is empty, she will open the car door and climb into the back seat. No one has come up with a good explanation for her strange quirk. When Glen picked her up during the summer of 1998, he drove silently for a few blocks, and could see her in his rearview mirror.

"She actually looked like a ghost," admits Glen, "but I thought she was just one of those 'goth' people. You know, the ones who wear a lot of white makeup and get those weird piercings. She was pretty, though, even as wet and pale as she was. I kept waiting for her to tell me where she wanted me to take her, but she just sat there silently. Finally, I just turned around to ask her, and I almost crashed my car when I saw that she had vanished. It was, like, instant because she disappeared in the millisecond I took my eyes off the rearview mirror and turned towards her. I had to stop my car after that, because my heart had started racing and I couldn't calm myself down. It was the strangest thing that ever happened to me."

It was a year later before Glen was willing to tell anyone what had happened that night, and to his shock, he discovered that his experience wasn't unique.

"I told a friend of mine, and she told me that something just like that had happened to her cousin. It was from her that I found out about how her ghost will only get into a car if there's only one person in it, because she had talked to a bunch of people who Donna's ghost refused to go with."

Glen has driven down 16th Avenue West many times since then, but he has yet to reencounter Donna's spirit.

"From what I've heard, once her ghost has had any sort of contact with you, then it'll never bother you again, because no one I've talked to who has seen it has seen it more than once."

Forever left on the corner of the University of British Columbia's 16th Avenue West with nowhere to go and no desire to stay, the fate of Donna Grainger is a good example to everyone that being rude and ill-tempered can lead you on a road you don't want to travel. Remembering what happened to her, consider that next time you find yourself about to tell someone to "shut up." Just take a deep breath and tell them that you "respectfully disagree." It just might save you a night spent out in the rain.

Silently

UNIVERSITY OF JUDAISM,
LOS ANGELES, CALIFORNIA

In 1947, Dr. Mordecai Kaplan, the author of the book *Judaism as a Civilization,* decided that the U.S. needed a school that would reflect the many forms of Jewish expression and culture. He called his new school the University of Judaism, and it immediately became the preeminent institution of its kind in North America. For 32 years the university moved around to various locations, until 1979 when it finally settled on its own campus in the wealthy Californian enclave known as Bel Air. Unfortunately for the school, an act of horrible violence that occurred during construction of the new campus has forever left a mark on its soccer field. Anyone who hears the story soon understands why men who walk on the field late at night during the autumn months find themselves at a loss for words.

Like many communities in California, it is vitally important to own a car in order to have fun. A sprawling community of expensive homes and grand estates, Bel Air is not a place designed for pedestrian accessibility. To be a teenager in Bel Air without a car is tantamount to a prison sentence, for without one, all of the malls and hangouts that are such an important part of teen culture are out of reach. Although many of the young people who live there are well-off enough to have their own vehicles, there are still the sad few who just have to make do. One way they accomplish the task is to designate spots in the community as hangouts. Places that are unlikely to attract noisy adults or burly policemen are always the most popular. In 1978, the place to be was the soccer field on the grounds of the University of Judaism, which at the time was still being built. To those who arrived at the field night after night for activities their parents would surely have disapproved of, it was a glorious length of grassy heaven. But, one damp, foggy October morning, all of that changed when a laborer working at the university construction site made a grisly discovery.

The girl's body was cold and lifeless, but her eyes were still open, staring accusingly at the gray sky. The police were called immediately, but there was little they could do besides cover her up and send her body to the morgue. The girl had no ID, and her fingerprints were not on file, so the tag that dangled from her toe read "Jane Doe."

Jane's autopsy revealed that her attacker had ensured that she would not have been able to tell anyone who he was: her tongue had been cut off, resulting in a thick mass of blood covering her face. The loss of blood from the wound was enough for the medical examiner to conclude that she had bled to death.

No one ever came to claim Jane's body, and her true identity was never revealed. It was hard for people to understand how this beautiful young girl with big brown eyes and long curly brown hair could be found dead on a field in one of the most well-to-do neighborhoods in North America and have no one looking for her. Without any conclusive evidence, the police were forced to file the case away, and Jane's body was unceremoniously disposed of.

The teenagers who had hung out at the park found a new place to party after that. Some came to visit the field after the police left, to satisfy their morbid curiosity, but there was little to see, and they soon stopped going. None knew who Jane was, and although some could get pretty wild, none was capable of the crime that had been committed and were immediately ruled out as suspects before the police gave up looking.

In September of the following year, the university opened its doors and classes began on the new campus. Students arrived from all over the country and swarmed the grounds with that mixture of hope, fear and exploration that comes over people as they take to a new place. Most, thrilled at the idea of going to school in the land of the warm Californian sun, were taken aback by the chilliness of the autumn night. One student, who repeatedly asked not to be identified, was rushing to his dorm room because the thin T-shirt he wore was doing little to protect him from the cold night air and the misty rain that had begun to sprinkle down. He was running across the soccer field, completely unaware of its history, when he suddenly came to a screeching halt. Standing at the other end of the field was a beautiful young woman. Normally, a lovely woman would have been enough to get his attention, but as she was also naked, it was all he could do to keep his eyeballs from popping out of their sockets. His

wonder turned to concern when he saw that she looked bewildered and confused. He ran over to her to ask if she was okay, but when he got there he found that, no matter how hard he tried, he could not make a sound. He stood right in front of her and watched as she tried to scream, but she too seemed to be rendered mute. Before he could do anything else, she finally appeared to notice him and immediately vanished from sight.

Understandably spooked, the frightened young man kept his bizarre story to himself, until he heard someone mention what had happened on the field the preceding year. Ashen-faced, he then described what he had seen. As he told his story, he realized that the young woman had been trying to scream out a name. It was quickly assumed that she was trying to call out the name of the man who killed her. But the young man was not a lip reader, so the murderer's identity remained hidden.

Over the two decades that have followed, a few similar sightings have been reported, but much more common are the stories of the strange effect the field has on men during September and October. It is said that, like the young man who first saw Jane's ghost that rainy night, any male who walks on the field late at night during those two months will find himself rendered mute.

There is a truth that for many is too horrible to contemplate. Every year the bodies of nameless men and women are found and never identified, even in this world of high-tech DNA magic. Although many of these people die of natural causes, such as exposure, or by their own hand, some are the victims of crimes that are by their nature destined to forever go unsolved. The beautiful young woman found on the soccer field on what would become the campus of the University of Judaism is not alone in her suffering. One can only imagine how many more anonymous spirits walk this earth after being robbed of the only two things every single living person has: a life and an identity. Even if by some miracle poor Jane were the only one, that still seems too many.

4

The Agonies
of Adolescence

Many people look back on their teenage years as the best time of their lives, but the ghosts that haunt the schools in this chapter would disagree. Forced to deal with loneliness, strict parents and their own insecurities and feelings of inadequacy, these students demonstrate what we call the agonies of adolescence.

A Snake in the Grass

Sometimes when a fatal accident occurs, the factors involved fit together so well that it's hard to believe that the incident was a matter of random chance, and one cannot help but use a word like fate. Sheena (whose name has been changed out of respect for her family's wishes) was a punk rocker. By today's standards her style would seem almost innocent and preppy. In 1985 her clothes and attitude were such that she was branded a rebel and troublemaker, even though her only act of rebellion was stealing the occasional smoke in the woods behind her high school, which was named after the small town where she lived, Newaygo, Michigan. Unfortunately, it was this one small, illicit act of teenage pleasure, along with one of her more quirky interests, that led to the moment that left her body lifeless and her spirit forever connected to the school she hated.

When she was 16, Sheena shocked everyone she knew by dying her blond hair jet black and styling it with a hazy cloud of hairspray, so that it stood on end in an ever-changing number of sharp spikes. Occasionally she would throw some purple or green highlights into the mix, just to shake things up. She didn't do it too often because the other kids made fun of her when she did, that is, when they weren't making fun of her clothes. At a bigger school, her appearance probably wouldn't have been noticed much, but at Newaygo there were no other similarly inclined outsiders for Sheena to bond with. Most people would give up looking like she did after a week of steady teasing and outright bullying, but Sheena was made of sterner stuff, and the taunting she received from her peers only strengthened her resolve to be nothing like them. Ever since she saw a story about British punks when she was just nine, she had dreamed that she would look like that and now that she had worked up the courage to make her dream a reality, she wasn't about to change back.

All her life she had felt different from the other boys and girls she grew up with. Her interests didn't mesh with the quietly religious culture of her hometown. From an early age she was obsessed with death and spent hours imagining what it would be like to die. She hadn't decided if she believed in an afterlife yet, so she wasn't sure if she saw death as an end or a beginning. She read books voraciously, and she developed a fascination for snakes and reptiles. There was something about their skin that she found comforting. And, when she was 14, she started smoking. She stole cigarettes from her father, who went through them so quickly there was no way he would ever notice that one or two were missing. There were other students at Newaygo High who smoked, but Sheena never joined them. Instead, she preferred to sit in the woods behind the school and smoke while she read from whatever book she was carrying around that day and listen to music on her Walkman.

On the last Monday of her life, she was reading a Kurt Vonnegut book, *Mother Night*. It was one of her favorites, and she had already read it about 10 times. On this day she had chosen to wear one of her most shocking ensembles, a black dress that she had cut apart and refitted

using staples and safety pins. With it she wore knee-high black socks and heavy, industrial black boots. She had decided to go with a lot of little spikes today, instead of three or four big ones, and she had randomly colored them red, blue, green and purple. Although it was only 11:00 AM she had already been called a freak 19 times. For some reason she always felt compelled to keep track of things like that. She refused to dwell on the number, and instead, focused on her book and took a long drag from a stolen cigarette.

She had been reading for about 10 minutes when, out of the corner of her eye, she saw something move in the grass. She lifted her head to see what it was. For just a moment, she saw the head of a medium-sized brown snake. Excited, she put down her book and approached the creature. She owned three snakes herself and had held many others, so she wasn't at all afraid. She knew that in Michigan there was only one known species of snake that was venomous, and that they were much too rare to worry about.

Compared to other rattlesnakes, the Eastern Massasauga Rattlesnake, at between 18 and 30 inches long, is the smallest and least venomous. The snake is not endangered, but it is protected by the state and is hard to find, and although poisonous, it prefers to flee a predator rather than attack. Sheena knew all about the rattlesnake, which was why she didn't think twice about approaching her slithering visitor. As she walked towards it, she didn't bother to take off her Walkman earphones. With the volume cranked up so loud, she failed to hear the telltale rattle that was her warning to stay away.

The snake began to slither away from her, but Sheena quickened her pace and grabbed hold of it. The snake did what instinct had programmed it to do and sunk its fangs deeply into her hand. Sheena swore and let the snake go. She held her hand and began to walk towards the school. The venom of the Eastern Massasauga Rattlesnake isn't as deadly as other rattlesnakes, but it didn't take long for Sheena to become nauseous and dizzy. She became disoriented and tripped over a large exposed tree root. When she fell she slammed her head against a large rock and knocked herself unconscious.

If she had made it back to the school, Sheena would have survived. Unfortunately, the time she spent lying on the ground was enough for the relatively weak poison to stop her heart. She was found dead the next day.

Many of her fellow students who had made her life so miserable attended her funeral. Her peers didn't say much at the funeral and even less when they returned to school. On the one hand, it was sad to have someone of the same age die, while on the other hand, no one knew her well enough to mourn her passing. It was because of this ambivalence that the first appearance of Sheena's ghost was free of the usual dramatics that usually coincide with such an encounter.

A group of students was standing behind the school, smoking and laughing, when they saw a girl with spiky hair in a strange black dress walk into the woods. They all knew who, or more accurately what, they had seen. As strange as it was, the only thing anyone could think of to say was "sheesh, she *would* come back as a ghost, wouldn't she?" Everyone nodded in agreement. Out of all the people at Newaygo High School, only Sheena was weird enough to try and haunt it.

From then on the woods behind the school have offered up frequent glimpses of Sheena's gothic-looking spirit. In death, as in life, she never interacts with anybody and has yet to do anything beyond hanging out. Some have wondered why she would choose to stay so close to the place she hated and near the people who made her so unhappy. One possible reason is that her time spent in those woods, reading, smoking and listening to music, was the happiest of her short life and she can think of no better way to wile away eternity. Another is that she may want to find that snake, not to kill it, but to tell it that she doesn't blame it for what happened.

Given all of the factors involved in Sheena's death, it is hard to describe it as a simple accident. It seems too great a coincidence that a young girl who loved snakes would come across one that had the distinction of being one of the rarest and only venomous snakes in Michigan. Add to that the loud music she loved causing her not to hear the one sign that could have spared her life, and you have to believe that, for whatever reason, Sheena was truly meant to die that day. Perhaps then, there is another reason why her ghosts haunts those woods behind her old school, a reason that will not be clear until her destiny is finally met.

Hollywood High

HOLLYWOOD, CALIFORNIA

Ever since the day the legendary director Cecil B. De Mille filmed his silent western *The Squaw Man* inside a barn in an undeveloped part of California, the stretch of land inside Los Angeles known as Hollywood has become synonymous with the art of turning dreams into realities. Every year, thousands of people arrive at this mecca of movie stardom, only to find a disturbingly rundown neighborhood overrun with homeless people and tacky tourist traps. Even then many refuse to let the humble drone of reality interfere with their dreams of glory, and they decide to stay and try everything it takes to get that audition that could lead to them becoming a household name. Only a tiny minority ever gets that chance, and only a select few achieve the fame that they desire, but for most the tiniest sliver of possibility is enough to keep them going.

Many dreamers are adults who are free to do whatever they like in their search for stardom, but others still have to go to school. For these young men and women there is a school ideally suited for their way of life; a school where the arts take precedent over the academics and where classes end early enough for everyone to get to auditions. Fittingly, the school is called Hollywood High, and over the years, it has amassed an alumni full of names easily recognizable from over 70 years of film and television. Mickey Rooney, Judy Garland, Lana Turner, Lon Chaney, Jr., and Fay Wray were all former students who left their mark in what is commonly referred to as Hollywood's Golden Age. Fans of TV from the 70s and 80s were glued to shows featuring former students like John Ritter, James Garner, Scott Baio, Carol Burnett and Mike Farrell. In the school's collection of yearbooks you can also find pictures of Oscar nominees and winners as diverse as Jason Robards, Keith Carradine and John Huston.

The school was built in 1910 to accommodate the children of the farmers who found themselves attracted to the land of dirt roads and lemon groves. Three years later De Mille shot Hollywood's first feature-length film. And it didn't take long after that for the then-normal house of learning to become an industry school. Many of its students were the sons and daughters of show biz's biggest names, which gave the school the reputation for having the most physically beautiful student body in the world. But as the neighborhood's glamour faded, the stars stopped sending their children to Hollywood High in favor of schools in more prestigious neighborhoods.

Still, for working students, Hollywood High was and is the place to go, because it allowed them to get an education and find work at the same time. There is often tension in the school, especially because some students are more successful than their peers. To see someone you know succeed, when you know in your heart that they are not nearly as talented as you are, can leave a bitter taste in your mouth. It is a taste that Hollywood High's best-known ghost knows well. Dumped by his girlfriend and tired of constantly losing jobs to students he saw every day, this young man left a mark on the school that has yet to be erased.

Known around the school as Tobe, the real name of this sad spirit is protected by the faculty and the former students who knew him, out of respect for his family. This ring of secrecy still hasn't prevented the story of his origin from becoming a part of the school's legend. Much of the story is vague, but the following represents the most likely version of events.

The year was 1955 and Tobe was a popular junior at the school. A child actor, he managed to find occasional work in television, but after he hit puberty most casting directors weren't interested in seeing him. He had been a cute kid, but his teenage features, sprinkled as they were with a hint of acne, were not what they were looking for. As a result, his mother, who was the worst stereotype of a stage parent, berated him all the time. She would yell at him for refusing to join in the humiliating stunts she thought up to get him back into the minds of the people that mattered, and she would ridicule him for not being as successful as some of his friends, whose more camera-friendly features got them small parts here and there.

Somehow Tobe managed to get through these tirades without lashing back at his mother, whose insults, he knew, were inspired more by her failures than his own. One of the things that allowed him to remain calm was the love he felt for his girlfriend, Svetlana. Lana, as all her friends called her, was a darkly beautiful girl whose parents had escaped from behind the Iron Curtain when she was an infant. Even at a school where many of the female students actually worked as professional models, Lana was said to stand out, reminiscent of a 15-year-old Ava Gardner. It was ironic that, given her charisma and beauty, she was one the school's few students who had absolutely no show-business aspirations. She went to Hollywood High because it was close to where she lived and its flexible hours allowed her to work part-time at a drug store to help her family. Tobe worshipped her, and thanks to her presence in his life, he was able to ignore the stress he had to deal with every day from his mother.

Unbeknownst to Tobe, Lana had caught the eye of his friend, Laurence, who along with sharply defined good looks also had a tenacity Tobe's mother constantly criticized her son for not possessing. Behind Tobe's back he began to talk to Lana at school and visit her at the store where she worked. Laurence was always charming and friendly and never said anything to her about Tobe, but his intentions were obvious. He even went so far as to befriend her parents and patiently listened to them as they struggled to have a conversation with him in English. It didn't take long for them to take to Laurence and not so subtly suggest that he was the type of young man she should be friends with. They had met Tobe and had thought him pleasant enough, but they decided that Laurence had a future. Tobe didn't.

Lana liked Tobe a lot, but at a time when many people got married just after high school, she had to admit that this other suitor made for the better prospect. As nicely and politely as she could, she told Tobe that they could just be friends and that was all. She felt so guilty when she saw the look of confused heartbreak on his face; she couldn't bear to tell him who she was leaving him for. Instead, she quietly got up and walked away.

As hurt as he was, it was the news that Lana was now seeing Laurence that sent Tobe over the edge. For the first time he really heard what his mother was saying and decided that she was right. The next day at school he could hear the murmur of whispers whenever he walked past a group of people. He knew what they were talking about and he couldn't take it any more. He skipped the rest of his classes and walked over to the school's auditorium, where he sat on the dark, empty stage and cried. He didn't go home that night. The next morning his lifeless body was found on the stage. He had hanged himself.

From the time of his death a shadowy figure began to appear in the auditorium. Doors started opening and closing by themselves. A loud, angry pounding could be heard in some of the more secluded areas of the school, and objects began to move about by themselves. Cursed, perhaps by the foolishness of his final action, Tobe's spirit remains at the school; a symbol of what not to do when the rejections that are an inevitable part of the Hollywood dream become too much to take.

It says something about the allure of that dream that so many people are willing to subject themselves to rejection to pursue it. Because of this allure, many of Hollywood High's students have to deal with stress and pressures, but they endure, and when the world feels too heavy, they have the example of their school's pathetic phantom as an example of the road not to take.

A Boy and His Instrument

PAOLA HIGH SCHOOL,
PAOLA, KANSAS

A person didn't have to know a lot about music to hear the effort it took Michael Sullivan to produce the notes he performed. But as inspiring as his intensity was, the passion with which he played only served to highlight the obvious—Michael could not play the trumpet. He could always get a sound out of it, but it wasn't anything a person would want to listen to. After suffering through the 17-year-old's attempts to play such classics as *Three Blind Mice* and *Hot Cross Buns,* his band teacher, Mr. Bava, would later insist that the boy was as untalented with the instrument as anyone, living or dead, could ever hope to be. When Michael died, Mr. Bava's words proved oddly prophetic. Michael's trumpet playing really was as bad after his death as it was during his life.

It all started at the beginning of September when Michael began his sophomore year at Paola High School in his hometown of Paola, Kansas. Paola is a small town, and like many small towns, is proud of the efforts of its local high school athletes, especially its football players. As in high schools all around North America, the boys who played for the Paola High Panthers were the kings of the school, ruling the campus with a cocky air of entitlement. They dated the prettiest girls and were treated royally by the town.

It was only natural then that virtually every boy would attend the tryouts held at the beginning of the year. So even though the head coach almost always had his team picked out by the end of the previous year, and it was pretty much impossible to impress him enough to change his mind, every boy on the field nearly killed himself in an often-foolish attempt to stand out.

Michael was 5' 6" and weighed 115 pounds. He stared out at the world wearing thick glasses, and when he tried to run for more than five minutes, he would hyperventilate. Most people like Michael would know that they were not designed to be football players. Their bodies were made for less physically rigorous events like chess and Mahjong. Before the tryouts were over, he was carried off the field on a stretcher with a bloody nose, a bruised rib and a possible concussion.

Like all of the other boys who didn't make the cut, Michael felt that he was doomed to spend the rest of his teen years as an unpopular loner. It was because of his despair that he made the decision that would mean his eventual doom: he joined the band.

Unlike the football team, there was no prestige in being associated with the band. A "band geek" instantly became a target for the football players who enjoyed playing games that involved stuffing the musicians into small spaces like lockers and garbage cans. Given these hazards, it is hard to understand how the band even managed to exist.

Maybe the students who joined were social lepers already, and they knew that nothing they did could make their situation any worse. At least now they had a bunch of similarly embattled peers with whom they could hang out and have fun. The band may have been the lowest clique on the totem pole, but at least it was still a clique. As well, it is possible that some genuinely loved to play music, and they didn't care what anybody thought. These brave few were the students who invariably sat first chair for their instruments because they were the ones who could actually play. The second and third chairs were reserved for those whose talents ranged from the middling to the told-to-just-pretend-they-were-playing.

Michael had no options other than band after being told he was too easy to beat to join the chess team, too incompetent for the AV squad, too wooden for the drama society and too unilingual for the French club. He had never even touched an instrument when he joined the band, which, to the chagrin of Mr. Bava, the music teacher, wasn't uncommon. So it was purely chance that he was handed a trumpet.

When he got home that day, he took the instrument out of its case and sat it down on his bed to look at it. It seemed so foreign and mysterious to him, but there was something appealing in its curves. He picked it up and ran his fingers along its cool, smooth surface. He found the feel of the brass comforting and safe. It looked and felt to him more like a work of art than a horn. He wanted to hear its music, so he put his lips to it and blew as hard as he could. The sound echoed throughout the house and scared his dog so badly that she stayed in her secret hiding spot for four hours. A rush of exhilaration surged through his body. From that first blast of noise, he knew that he had found the instrument of his destiny.

Michael practiced every day. And eventually, he mastered the fingering of all the assigned songs, which meant that as bad as he was, a person could still, with effort, identify the tunes he was playing.

The more he played, the more convinced Michael became that he was meant to play. Soon he began to dream of sitting first chair and playing a solo. He shrugged off Mr. Bava's suggestions that he was tone deaf, ignored his parents' threats to send him to military school and daydreamed happily while the football players stuffed him into small and confined spaces. He was so sure of himself that no one had the heart to tell him to stop, no matter how much they wanted him to.

As time went on Michael's drive began to alienate him from the other band members. Daniel Kreskin, the young man lucky enough to play first chair trumpet, was by far the most popular member of the band. A charismatic leader, he was the only person who managed to bridge the divide between the jocks and the "band geeks." If he had wanted to, Daniel could have played for the football team;

the coach had told him so. But he chose to join the band. In turning down inevitable football glory, Daniel had made his fellow band mates feel special and worthy. If he wanted to be in the band, they decided that being a band member must be something worth being.

Michael despised Daniel and saw him only as an obstacle in his path. Having finally risen to second chair, a promotion made possible only by his incessant nagging of Mr. Bava, Michael dreamed that something bad would happen to Daniel. Nothing ever did.

For two long years Michael sat in the second chair and not once did he ever get to play a solo. At each concert, the sound of Daniel playing beside him felt like an ice pick being stabbed into his eardrum. His bitterness grew, and his malicious fantasies became more violent in their execution.

As homecoming approached, the band began to practice in the football field for the halftime show. Although they were not a marching band, Mr. Bava liked to give them a chance to feel the open air and get used to the autumn chill that could take a toll on their fingers. Since the football players used the field after school, the only time they had access to it was early in the morning before school started. Mr. Bava was not a morning person and was even more irritable than usual during these practices. He was also more forgetful as the caffeine from his first coffee had yet to reach his brain. Because of his forgetfulness, for the last practice before the big game, he had forgotten to bring the special homecoming shirts that the band traditionally wore on the big day. They were packed away in two boxes in the storage room above the gym.

Knowing that the first rule of teaching was "never lift any-thing if you can get a student to do it," he asked Daniel and Michael to go and get the shirts.

By this time, Michael had managed to become just what he had feared before he joined the band—a pariah. Angered by Michael's arrogance and his hostility towards Daniel, the other members of the band only spoke to him when it was impossible to avoid it. Ironically, the only person who still talked to him was Daniel, who was too nice to be offended by Michael's attitude. And when everyone talked about Michael behind his back, Daniel was the only person who ever defended him. If Michael had known of Daniel's support, it would have only made him hate Daniel more. As they walked towards the gym, Daniel tried to engage Michael in polite small talk, but he failed to get any response. He pretended not to notice and chatted one-sidedly until they reached their destination.

The only way to get to the storage space above the gym was by climbing up a steep stairway by the right-hand bleachers. Daniel ran up the steps, while Michael strug-gled to get to the top. When they walked into the room, they were surprised to find that it was a mess. Items of every description were thrown about at random, and it was only by chance that Daniel managed to spot the two boxes marked "Band Shirts." After they moved the junk that blocked their way, Daniel handed Michael one of the boxes and picked up the other one himself.

At that moment, Michael realized he was in a situation that closely resembled one of the violent fantasies he had daydreamed for the past two years. After all that time dealing with his hatred and his jealousy, Michael was no longer able to dismiss the thought. The poor boy snapped.

As Daniel headed towards the door, Michael put down his box and pretended to tie his shoelace. He waited until Daniel was out of sight, then stood up and ran to the stairway. His plan was simple. He would push Daniel down the stairs and become first chair. But he hadn't counted on Daniel going down the stairs as quickly as he did. By the time Michael got to the door, Daniel was only a few steps away from the floor. He also hadn't counted on his actually untying his own shoelace while he pretended to tie it. As he ran out of the storage room door, he tripped on the dangling shoelace and tumbled headfirst down the stairs.

Daniel had taken a first aid course, but there was nothing he could do. Michael was dead before he hit the gym floor. His neck was broken.

That year's homecoming was dedicated to Michael, although most of the people who attended the game and the dance had no idea who he was. The band wore black armbands while they played, and Daniel, elected homecoming king, gave a tearful speech honoring his fallen second chair.

That might have been the last anyone at the school thought about Michael, if it were not for his insane determination. Michael was so dedicated to becoming first chair that he refused to let a matter as trivial as his death get in his way.

As the days and weeks passed, the sound of a badly played trumpet could be heard throughout the school. At first, people assumed that it was just a "band geek" practicing, but all of the band's trumpet players insisted that the only time they practiced in school were during band rehearsals. Whenever the students heard the trumpeter, they searched, but couldn't find the source of the music.

It was Mr. Bava who first speculated that it was Michael. He, more than anyone, knew how much Michael wanted to be first chair. The thought that the boy would return from the dead to do so didn't surprise him.

Soon the novelty of the phantom trumpeter grew thin, and people stopped noticing him. It was only at the beginning of each September, as new students came to the school, that his presence was ever mentioned. The new students would talk excitedly about him for about a week, before they too grew tired of him. He didn't seem to care. No one noticed him when he was alive, so it hardly mattered if they didn't notice him when he was dead.

Eventually Paola High moved out of the old building and into new, more modern facility. Michael did not move with it. Instead, he stayed at the old building and can be heard there still, committing unspeakable musical crimes with his trumpet. As the years pass, he continues practicing. He never gets better and he never will. Perhaps it is a blessing that on that fateful day he wasn't handed a tuba.

The Clock Tower

When the city planners in the town of Port Chester, New York, decided to build a high school, they must have wanted to subconsciously implant in its students the will to aim for the highest reaches of public office. That may explain why Port Chester High School, with its six Roman columns and high clock tower, looks like a conglomeration of some of Washington, DC's most famous buildings. It is possible that the school was merely the result of the architectural trends of the period in which the school was built, but it is obvious that the people who built Port Chester High wanted to create a building that would excite the imaginations of its students. And along with a hardworking and dedicated faculty, Port Chester High is the school of every parent's dreams. Free of so many of the problems that plague other schools, students were able to focus on the one thing they're actually there for—their education. But this has not always been the case. Decades earlier, Port Chester High was forced to come to grips with a problem that had gone ignored for years, until it resulted in the death of a student and the haunting of the school's clock tower.

Although hazing is most often associated with colleges and universities, it has also become an annual high school ritual. In the case of Port Chester High, though, the people being hazed are not voluntary participants who want to become a part of a group. Instead they are students whose only crime was starting the 10th grade. Like many other schools, there was a time at Port Chester High when being a freshman during the first month of classes was an open invitation to any number of potentially painful and embarrassing situations. There were two reasons for this tradition. The first was that all of the upperclassmen had been forced to undergo the same painful experience, and they didn't think it was fair to spare the newcomers. And there were other students who were just bullies at heart, accounting for the second reason the tradition existed—they just liked to hurt people.

In 1947, Timothy O'Herlihy had just started the 10th grade. A slight boy with red hair and freckles, he was smart and liked to take things apart and put them back together again. He loved comic books and had yet to discover girls, even though many had begun to hover close to him. Not conventionally handsome, Timothy had a strange charisma that many found inviting, and he made friends easily. He looked forward to starting high school, seeing it as a chance to get to know new people and learn new things. In his first week at Port Chester High, he already had a crowd of people around him who listened to him intently when he talked about serious matters and who laughed happily when he repeated jokes he'd heard on the radio. It was because of his instant popularity that he was, at first, spared the ritual freshman hazing. Many of the upperclassmen liked him too much to hurt him, and others were afraid that doing something to him would have a negative impact on their own social status. So by the time the last day of hazing month arrived, Tim had gotten away unscathed.

Unfortunately for Tim, his escape had not gone unnoticed. A group of three boys named Jerry, Sam and Emil realized, as the last hour of hazing month began, that Tim could get away scot-free. With just 55 minutes left on the clock, they decided to act swiftly and rectify the situation. In time they would forever regret the rashness of their actions.

As the students walked through the halls on their way to the last class of the day, the three young men strained to find Tim in the crowd. Luckily, they were able to spot him. Emil approached him and struck up a conversation about the latest issue of Action Comics, a topic that Tim was only too happy to discuss. As they talked, the crowds in the hallways began to thin out and eventually only Tim and the three boys were left. Tim was expounding on the glories of Superman, while Jerry and Sam, who had been pretending to be engrossed in a conversation of their own, sneaked up behind Tim and grabbed him.

Tim began to struggle, but the three boys were larger than he was and he soon realized that there wasn't much use. The problem for Emil, Jerry and Sam was that now that they had him, they had no idea what to do to him. They knew it had to be something big to make up for all the days that he had gone home untouched, but they couldn't think of what that could be. They ducked into a broom closet and brainstormed while Tim patiently waited for them to make up their minds. He knew how lucky he had been over the past month and had accepted his fate as inevitable.

Finally, Emil came up with an idea.

"We could dangle him out of the clock tower," he suggested.

Sam and Jerry both agreed enthusiastically to the plan. Tim, on the other hand, began to protest. Of all the possible ideas, none could have scared him more. Ever since his father had taken him up to the top of the Empire State Building during a family trip to New York City, Tim had suffered from a terrible fear of heights, or more accurately, a fear of hitting the ground after falling from a height. The thought of being dangled from the high tower was enough for him to try to claw and bite his way out of his captors' arms. His struggling only made it clear to the boys that they had come up with the perfect prank, and they carried the terrified freshman out of the broom closet and up the steps to the tower, which was actually off limits to students.

As they moved closer to the tower, Tim grew more violent in his attempts to escape, but his struggles only made the three boys angry and they held onto him even more tightly. Finally, they got to the top of the tower and they opened up a window. Tim began to cry as they lifted him up, only proving to Sam, Jerry and Emil that this hazing would easily be worth what they had gone through. As they pushed him out through the window headfirst holding onto his legs, Tim began to scream hysterically for help. His obvious fear was enough to satisfy them, so they began to pull him back in. But as they did, Jerry slipped towards the window and lost his grip, causing him to bump into Sam, who also lost his grasp of the screaming boy. All it took was that one second for all of Tim's weight to be put into Emil's hands, which were not strong enough bear it. To their horror, Tim plummeted to the concrete below. Without thinking, they ran out of the tower as fast as they could and out of the school. They couldn't bring themselves to see if Tim was still alive, and it was only later in the day that they heard from other students that their victim had not survived his hazing.

Despite all evidence to the contrary, Tim's death was ruled a suicide, and Jerry, Sam and Emil swore to each other that they would never tell a soul what really happened. They did their best to pretend that everything was normal and tried to forget that they had killed someone, but as the months passed signs appeared suggesting that some kind of supernatural force was not going to let them off easily.

Emil was the first one to see the ghostly figure of Timothy. He was playing basketball in gym class when, out of the corner of his eye, he spotted the angry-looking phantom. Stunned, he turned to face the floating figure, only to have the ball slam directly into his face, breaking his nose.

Jerry saw the ghost next in a science lab. He was working on a chemistry experiment when he saw Tim's ghost standing right beside his lab partner. He jumped away from the spirit and caught the sleeve of his sweater on the flame of his Bunsen burner. It caught on fire, but he was able to get it out before it caused serious damage.

When Sam saw it, he was in the woodshop. The sight of the transparent apparition caused him to slam his thumb with a hammer. His thumbnail eventually fell off, but it never grew back.

Soon the three boys began to see the ghost all the time. The sight of the poor boy staring angrily at them was more than they could take. When school ended for the year, they hoped that summer holidays would offer them a respite from his visitations, but they were wrong. By the time school began again, they couldn't go anywhere without encountering Tim's vengeful spirit. The hauntings proved too much for Emil, and he shot himself. His suicide was the final straw for Sam and Jerry, and they decided to confess their role in Tim's death. After hearing the story, both the school and the police decided that it would be best for the community not to press charges. Instead of sending the two guilt-stricken boys to prison, officials instead banned the practice of hazing freshman.

Sam and Jerry continued to see Tim even after they were absolved of their crime. When they graduated, both left Port Chester to join different branches of the military. Neither ever returned.

The ghost of Timothy O'Herlihy is said to still reside at Port Chester High. Over the years, the sad specter has been spotted inside the clock tower from which he fell. It has been seen opening and closing the tower's door, as if it wants to leave but cannot. His spirit serves as a reminder of what can happen when people insist on observing a tradition of cruelty. It took his death to show Port Chester High and the community at large that the practice of hazing freshman wasn't as innocent as they thought it was. It is sad to think that it took such a tragic accident to teach such a simple lesson.

5

Unsolved Mysteries

Although most of the incidents in this book can be understood and explained, those described in this chapter are much more enigmatic. They leave so many questions unanswered that we have no choice but to consider them unsolved mysteries.

The Order of the Gownsman

UNIVERSITY OF THE SOUTH,
SEWANEE, TENNESSEE

Located in the small town of Sewanee, Tennessee, the University of the South first opened its doors to students on September 18, 1868. At that time the school tried to offer up courses in fields as diverse as dentistry, engineering and law, but as the cost of those programs became prohibitive, they were dropped. The focus of the university shifted to undergraduate degrees in the arts and sciences and graduate degrees in theology. Boasting one of the most beautiful campuses in the South, if not on the continent, the school takes pains to bolster that beauty by tenaciously holding onto its more archaic traditions.

The most famous of these traditions is the Order of the Gownsmen. Reserved only for those students with the highest grade point averages, the members of this order are given the privilege of wearing long black robes not unlike those traditionally worn by students at British universities such as Oxford and Cambridge. Worn as badges of honor, these gowns earn their wearers the respect of the school population, and political power as well. Because of their influence, its members can help enact changes in policy that affect not only the order, but also the student population as a whole. As a result, some students resent the order and try their best to undermine it whenever they can. Although anyone with good enough grades can become a member, for some the order has the air of an exclusive secret society.

For many years this feeling has been supernaturally reinforced by the presence of a ghost whose true origin is shrouded in mystery. Known as the Headless Gownsmen, the phantom has been seen as both a floating, or in some cases, bouncing head and as a headless body dressed in the order's customary black robe. The ghost has no qualms about appearing in front of any student, but it is strongly suspected that it remains on campus to torment fellow members of the order.

There are currently two widely differing explanations for the origin of this disconnected wraith, but the majority of students on campus find both stories suspicious and unsatisfying. There is a distinct feeling that by offering these unlikely stories, the order is attempting to hide the real, and possibly sinister, truth.

The first version is the most obviously fictitious of the two. It tells of a young seminary student who was a member of the order. So obsessed with the pursuit of knowledge that he ignored all other activities in favor of studying. He often risked his health and his sanity by not eating and sleeping if they got in the way of his reading. According to the story, the young man was so focused on his work that he failed to notice that a long red rash had appeared around his neck. Too busy to ever talk to his fellow students, no one ever got a chance to ask him about it, thus warning him of its existence. As the weeks passed, the rash only got worse and soon became infected. He absentmindedly scratched the rash on occasion to relieve what he perceived was a vague itching sensation, but he still took no notice of it, even as the infected tissue began to turn green and ooze unpleasant fluids. By then it was too late. Even if he did notice, the infection was too far gone to be treated. The story ends with the young man's dead body found slumped over some books at his desk. His head was found on the floor next to him, where it had rolled after it had fallen off.

At first glance, the second version of the story may seem more plausible, but given the history of the ghost's appearances it is probably just as unlikely as the first. It tells of a young student who felt that his greatest achievement in life was when he was admitted into the Order of the Gownsmen and allowed to wear the black robe to classes. He was so proud of being a member that he went further than his peers and wore the robe not to just his classes and school functions, but everywhere. Some students even claimed he slept in it. It was rumored that he was so obsessed with the robe that he never took it off, but the robe was always impeccably clean and did not exude any of the strong odors that would have come from never being laundered. The truth was that he only wore it when he was out in public, but since that was the only time anyone ever saw him, it was easy to understand where these stories originated.

One night he went to visit his parents to show off the robe. To get there required driving along the narrow and winding road on Monteagle Mountain. The road required drivers to be extremely cautious and constantly vigilant, since you could easily drive off it and plummet to your death. The young man had driven along the road many times, but he was still never completely comfortable doing so. To make matters worse, it had begun to rain. As the water began to pour down, he reached over to switch on his windshield wipers. As he lifted his arm up, the sleeve of his robe caught on his gearshift, causing him to lurch to the right and accidentally turn the steering wheel. The car swerved on the wet road, and before he could react, the car went over the edge. When the wreckage was found, it was discovered that the force of the crash had severed the boy's head from his body.

Although this story is much more believable than the first, it is easily discounted by reports that the ghost first began to appear as far back as 1880, making the account of an automobile accident chronologically impossible. With the true account of the phantom's existence still unknown, all the students of the University of the South can be assured of is that sightings of the Headless Gownsmen have not diminished over the years. If anything, sightings have become more frequent and disturbing.

Seen most often around Wyndcliff and St. Luke's Halls, the strange specter has also visited every other building in the area. Most reports describe the presence of the ghost's headless body, but during final exam week it is much more likely for a student to come upon the spirit's floating head. Mute and expressionless, the head looks as though it once belonged to a man in his early 20s. Some have insisted that a visitation from the floating head during finals is a sure sign of academic doom, although others have argued just the opposite, that seeing the head is an omen of good grades in your future. The discord suggests that seeing the Gownsman's head actually has no bearing on how well a person does on an exam, but instead, offers a good excuse for unexpected failure or achievement.

The disembodied head is most frequently described as floating in the air in grand defiance of the laws of gravity, but it has also been seen to move about in a less-dignified manner. One student, who had fallen asleep late at night in Wyndcliff Hall while trying to study for a mid-term exam, was awakened by the sound of loud thumps coming from the staircase. The thumps were slow and methodical and unlike anything the student had ever heard before. He decided to investigate. What he saw was so bizarre that he had to pinch himself to prove that he wasn't dreaming. There on the steps he saw the school's famous disembodied head bouncing purposefully up the stairs, as if it was on its way to meet the body it had been separated from all those years ago.

As a place of tradition, beauty and high standards, Tennessee's University of the South is unique among the many schools that dot the North American landscape. Perhaps because of the school's renown, one of the world's most famous modern playwrights, Tennessee Williams, donated the rights to his entire body of work to the small university in Sewanee. With his plays he documented a time in the South that seems as distant now as the Earth is from the Moon, but thanks to the traditions the university has insisted on upholding, there is at least a place where a sense of that time period can still be found. Today the idea of wearing a black robe to class would seem as absurd as showing up in your pajamas. However, at the University of the South it is a mark of honor that comes with the burden of occasional mistrust and derision. There's a chance that the people smart enough to be permitted to wear those black robes are just as mystified about the identity of their school's famous headless spirit as anyone else. But as long as they exert some control over the student populace, they will always be suspected of knowing more.

Filling Up Quick

CRYSTAL PARK SCHOOL, GRANDE PRAIRIE, ALBERTA

One of the great mysteries of the supernatural is the way that certain buildings seem to attract ghosts while others do not. It seems logical that the number of ghosts a building contains would have something to do with how old it is. The truth is that there are buildings hundreds of years old that are completely free of phantoms, and yet there are buildings like Crystal Park School in Grande Prairie, Alberta, that have existed only for a couple of decades and have already amassed a surprisingly large collection of spirits. Built in 1984, this elementary-junior high school, which offers both regular and special needs classes, is home to at least four humanoid apparitions and a vast collection of nameless gray vapors.

The first of the human-shaped phantoms is an unknown couple who has been sighted emerging from a statue inside the school. They are always seen holding hands, and their transparent bodies emit a sickly, bluish-white glow that is reminiscent of a slowly dying fluorescent light bulb. One reason no one has been able to identify these spirits is because their faces look as though they have been damaged in some way. Without knowing how the couple died, it has been difficult to determine the cause of their disfigurement, but the most likely possibilities are a car accident, a fire or possibly both. Also unknown is their relationship to the statue, which has been at the school since it opened. One theory is that the sculptor made it for his wife as a token of his love and died with her in an accident before he could give it to her. Another is that the person who was responsible for the couple's death may have once owned the statue. But by far the most creative theory is that the man was married and having an affair with his ghostly partner. When his wife found out about the affair, she arranged their deaths and hired a witch to ensure the couple would spend the rest of eternity inside the statue her husband had bought for her as an anniversary present. All three theories are pure speculation, and the true origin of the phantom couple is a mystery that may never be solved.

Unlike these enigmatic spirits, the school's third ghost is much easier to explain. Bright blue, hardworking and transparent, this ghost used to work at the school as a janitor before an accident claimed his life. He died when he fell from the 30-foot platform that the custodians used when cleaning the school windows. His injury wouldn't have been fatal, but the accident unfortunately occurred at night during the week before Labor Day when no one else was around. If someone had been able to take him to a hospital as soon as he fell, he would have easily survived. He lay there the whole night, and by the time he was discovered, he had bled to death. Still, he bears the school no grudge. He doesn't even seem to acknowledge that anything bad happened to him and can be seen going about his duties late at night when the school is quiet and empty.

As easily identifiable as the janitor, the fourth ghost used to teach first grade at the school, when it first opened. Universally thought to be an excellent teacher, her only quirk was her habit of stopping in mid-sentence and staring out of one of her classroom windows, as if she was waiting for someone to arrive. As strange as her behavior was, no one ever felt comfortable asking her about it, so there exists a host of theories for her strange behavior. The most popular rumor was that her husband had left one night to go out for some cat food and never returned, and that she was always looking out the window in the hopes that she would see him coming back to her. The other theory was that she was not Canadian as she had claimed, and that in the 60s, she had taken part in an act of radical student protest in the U.S. so was wanted by the FBI. When she died suddenly and unexpectedly of a heart attack, another much more macabre theory took hold—she knew she was going to die at a young age and was constantly looking out for the angel of death in the hopes that she could avoid him. Of course, she couldn't. One thing that sets her ghost apart is that no one has ever seen her from inside the school. The only way to catch a glimpse of her spirit is to be standing outside, where she can be spotted staring back at you from out of a window.

The other spirits at Crystal Park School have no stories to tell, or if they do, there is no way to know what they may be. Found usually in the early morning hours, these ghosts take the form of a floating gray mist that could easily be confused with a patch of fog or smoke, if they were outside. No one knows why these vapors are attracted to the school.

Perhaps someday someone will figure out why the dead feel such a connection to a school that isn't even 20 years old. Hopefully when they do, they will also be able to answer many of the questions that these spirits raise. Until then, the ghosts of Grande Prairie's Crystal Park School will remain intriguing mysteries surrounded only by unproven gossip and rumors.

The Pact

DUNDAS DISTRICT PUBLIC SCHOOL, DUNDAS, ONTARIO

Only two incidents have occurred in the 70-year-old history of the Dundas District Public School in Dundas, Ontario, that could account for the strange sounds and practical jokes that plague the custodians who work there late at night. But the most dramatic of these incidents may well be a red herring that overshadows the more likely, yet less obvious, cause. Unlike other schools, Dundas' violent past may have little to do with its ghosts, and the school could be haunted simply because a group of men once made a pact.

It was a cold Christmas night in 1934 just five years after the school had been built, when a horrific accident forced the school to serve a very gruesome purpose. Dundas District was built close to an escarpment that trains from the local station frequently passed. That holiday night the combination of technical and human error caused two trains to collide right beside the school. Eighteen people were found dead in the wreckage that ensued. The town was not yet equipped with a hospital, so the dead were taken to the school basement, turning it temporarily into the Dundas morgue. This unusual double duty would, at first glance, seem to account for the strange incidents that occur frequently throughout the school. It isn't difficult to imagine the spirits of the corpses becoming attached to the place in which their remains were held. For a brief time, the morgue story was the popular explanation for the inexplicable incidents that occurred, until a group of former custodians admitted to once making a promise.

The year was 1954, and the five men who worked as custodians at the school were a close-knit, hardworking crew. Of the five, it was Russell who stood out. He was responsible for taking care of the third floor, and he took his job very seriously, treating it like it was the floor of a palace. Despite his perfectionism, he also had a reputation as a practical joker, because of the tricks he loved to play on his co-workers. The other men tolerated his prankish side because his jokes were never cruel and because they allowed the men to let off some steam by getting him back. According to the group's foreman, John (who has requested that his last name be withheld), it was Russell who came up with the idea that the five should make a vow.

"I've been thinking," Russell announced as the men sat down to lunch.

"That's new. How's it working out for you?" interrupted John with a sly grin.

Russell smiled before he continued, "I was thinking about how much I'm going to miss making you guys look like dopes. I don't know about you, but my favorite part of the day is always the moment when one of you realizes that I got you good. It's even better than quitting time as far as I'm concerned."

John shook his head.

"You got it all wrong, Russ," he insisted. "The best part of the day comes after one of us discovers whatever lame attempt at a joke you've tried that day, and we conspire to make you look like the fool you are."

"Exactly!" Russell laughed with a twinkle in his eyes. "That's why I think we should make a promise to ensure that we can keep up the fun even after we're gone."

The other men looked at him with confused expressions on their faces.

"What I'm suggesting is that we make a pact. The first one of us to die has to come back to the school and haunt the others!"

The others thought his idea was grim, but since none was planning on dying anytime soon, they humored him, shaking hands and agreeing to the pact.

Years passed, and the crew eventually split up. Only Russell and John stayed in Dundas, although John left the school for a different job in 1972. By then the pact that they had made was all but forgotten. Russell, by now the only member of the original crew, was the only one who really remembered it, and he still took it seriously. As it turned out, he was the first of the five to pass away. A heart condition took him when he was still relatively young.

In 1996, Veronika Lessard was hired as a custodian at Dundas District. She was assigned to work on the third floor, the area that had previously been Russell's domain.

When she first started no one mentioned to her that she might notice some strange occurrences during the course of an average shift. So she was unprepared when one night she went downstairs to have something to eat and came back to find that the floor she had intended to wash when she got back now appeared to be freshly mopped. Veronika was more grateful not to have to do the work than she was scared by its being done, but she still felt the need to relate the incident to her co-workers. It was then that they told her about Russell.

Strange things had started happening around the school just days after Russell died. For awhile they assumed the incidents had something to do with the train accident from all those decades ago, but when John heard about what was happening and told everyone about the pact, they realized that Russell had made good on his vow.

Other incidents that have Russell's mark on them include the time Veronika and her fellow custodian Tony Vermeer heard a voice at the top of the stairs. It sounded like an old woman, panicky and weak, begging for their help. Knowing that the school was empty and just about to leave, they hotfooted it out of the building without even bothering to check out the woman's cries. Later on they discovered that one of Russell's favorite tricks was to imitate the cries of a helpless woman or child and have people rush towards the sound.

During one March break, Veronika was on a ladder cleaning some lights in room 305 when she heard the clanking of keys beneath her. At first she assumed it was Tony, but when she called down to him, there was no answer. After a couple of minutes, Tony did come into the room, but when quizzed about his earlier appearance, insisted that this was the first time he'd been in the classroom that day. As he spoke, they could once again hear the sound of clanking keys. Veronika slid down her ladder and saw the shadowy figure of a tall, thin man. It jangled its keys and smiled at her before it walked out of the room and vanished.

Ever since motion detectors and security equipment have been installed in the school, there have been several instances of the devices going off for no earthly reason. The most dramatic of these incidents turned the school's principal, Peter Greenberg, from a skeptic into a believer. Principal Greenberg arrived at the school early one Saturday morning to catch up on some paperwork. When he got there, a guard who worked for the security company that oversaw the school informed him that the motion detector had been set off. The police arrived and began to search the building. They found no evidence of an intruder and left. Principal Greenberg, who had left to get some breakfast while the police went through the school, returned and went to his office. He had just started to get some work done when he heard the sounds of lockers opening and slamming shut. He called the police, and they came back right away. When they arrived, they heard the sounds of the lockers and of glass breaking on the third floor. It sounded as though a group of kids was tearing the school apart. Together Principal Greenberg and the police proceeded to the third floor. The noise seemed to be coming from one classroom. One of the officers took out his can of pepper spray and ordered the principal to stand behind him. With one arm out-stretched and ready to spray any violent offenders, he used the other to open the door. The noise stopped immediately. Principal Greenberg and the police were shocked to find that the room was empty and completely untouched. Russell, it seemed, had struck again.

If it was Russell, that is. For, despite all the evidence suggesting that his ghost is responsible for all the strange things that happen at the school, many have difficulty forgetting about the train wreck on Christmas day in 1934. Although the story of Russell's pact is the best explanation for what has happened at Dundas over the years, some still insist that the spirits of the dead bodies who spent the night in the school's basement have a much better excuse to remain at the school. One thing that becomes clear as more similar stories are researched is that violence, whether it is deliberate or accidental, is a powerful motivator of the supernatural. Russell's story is the more rational, but that doesn't mean it is the most likely. Without more evidence, opinions will remain divided, and the truth about who really haunts the Dundas District Public School will remain what it is today, a mystery.

This Train Don't Stop Here Anymore

TENNESSEE HIGH SCHOOL, BRISTOL, TENNESSEE

It isn't uncommon for strangers passing through Bristol, Tennessee, for the first time to assume that the long two-story red brick building with Roman columns at its front entrance is an old college or university. They are usually surprised to find the words Bristol Tennessee High School just above those ornate columns. Of all the high schools mentioned in this book, Tennessee High School is easily one of the most beautiful. It has a Southern grace indicative of the era in which it was built, a time when public buildings were built to be admired, just as much as they were to serve a bureaucratic purpose. Built in 1939, it has, over the last 60 years, come to serve as home to three distinct ghosts. Two are former students, a boy and a girl, who failed to graduate because they died, and the other is of an inanimate object whose presence at the school defies all rational explanation.

Of the two human ghosts, it is the boy who is the least likely to be seen. His appearances have thus far proved too rare for his spirit to be given a nickname by the staff and students, even though his real name has been lost to time. Usually assumed to be a student from the Fifth Street School, an earlier incarnation of Tennessee High, he is said to look like a burly athlete. Seen always around the field house, he still bears the wounds of the car accident that took his life. Usually spotted just before or after a school sports event, this ghost differs from his female counterpart in that he is more likely to appear in front of a group than an individual. These appearances are said to begin and end so quickly that most people aren't even aware that they occurred.

On the other hand, Agnes, Tennessee High's second ghost, isn't shy about making her presence felt. Over the years she has been both seen and heard throughout the building, usually at night when the building is almost empty. One night a drama student spotted her after a performance in the school auditorium. The play had ended several hours previously, but the boy had stayed to help clean up and strike the set. He was ready to leave, but had to retrieve some work from his locker first. As he walked through the quiet empty hallways, he turned a corner and saw a beautiful girl dressed in white walking towards him. She looked as though she was dressed for some sort of school formal, and her hair was bobbed in a style that the student recalled from old black and white movies. He smiled at her as she approached and nodded his head in greeting. She smiled back and walked past him. As she did, the young man was overtaken by the smell of chlorine. He turned to look at her and was shocked to see that she had vanished. It was then that he remembered the stories he had heard about Agnes, a young girl who was found floating in the school's pool the morning after Class Night, a Tennessee High tradition in which the school's seniors say goodbye to the school and promote the juniors into their place. How or why she had drowned was never solved, which may explain why her ghost remains at the school.

For years her footsteps could be heard late at night, until finally the hallways were carpeted and her steps were muffled. The janitorial staff still reported that they could often feel her presence, especially during the weeks before and after Class Night.

There is another legend regarding Agnes' death, which involves her being hit by a train while driving her car to Class Night. Although several well-known paranormal researchers have adopted this version of the story, they do not base the theory on fact. But the story allows for a more logical explanation of the school's third ghost, a phantom train that has been spotted racing out of the auditorium, through the hallway and into the old gymnasium. An old steam engine, the ghost train moves and shakes with such ferocity that it is said to shake the entire the school. The theory that the phantom train is the one that killed Agnes on that fateful night makes its manifestation more intuitively acceptable, but there is no evidence that the two ghosts are at all related. A more likely explanation for the spectral locomotive is simply that the school may have been built on a spot that the train once passed through.

Either way, Tennessee High's ghost train serves as an interesting departure from the more typical ghosts found inside the schools in this book, unlike Agnes and the unnamed athlete. As tragic as their stories are, they serve as a palpable reminder that as different as schools are everywhere, they still share accidents and occurrences that join them together in a bond of unrepentant humanity.

The Return of Miss Suzette

FOURTH WARD SCHOOL, VIRGINIA CITY, NEVADA

Considering its size and population, Virginia City, Nevada, may well be the most haunted place in North America. The site of what was one of the world's largest silver mines, this quaint little town was once known as the "Richest Place on Earth." Today it is mostly a tourist town, where people come from all over to revisit a past that is at once alien and reassuring. Great care has been taken to preserve the grand architecture of the town, and its buildings have a beautiful Victorian grace that must bring comfort to the spirits from yesteryear who inhabit them. The most charming of these historic structures is the Fourth Ward School, which has long had a reputation for housing phantoms. Given Virginia City's reputation for the supernatural, it isn't shocking that one can look out one of the building's windows and see another famous haunted spot. Visible outside is a shaft of the Comstock Mine, which was once home to the vengeful spirit of Henry Comstock, the man for whom the mine was named.

Along with its memorable view, the three-story building looks like a girl's dream dollhouse that has been magically transformed to life-size. The eye immediately focuses on the combination of the red paneling that surrounds its doors and windows and the blinding whiteness of its façade. In a strange way, the school has the pallor of a romantically gothic spirit. It looks as though the entire

building could begin to fade from sight at anytime or that a person could walk up to it and put a hand through the wall as if it wasn't there. Built in 1876, it was meant to hold 1000 students in grades 1 to 12. It was equipped with 16 large classrooms and two large study halls, and it served the community well for 60 years before it was closed in 1936. It sat empty for a few years until it was turned into a museum that is highlighted with pride in all of Virginia City's tourist literature. Among the people who visit the museum every year are scores of paranormal enthusiasts who are attracted to the building's abnormally high population of floating orbs, which many believe are the spirits of the students and faculty who died while the school was still operational.

Among those who have documented these fascinating phenomena are Byron and Dawn Smith, who, along with noted Nevada ghost researcher Janice Oberding, toured the building armed with cameras and caught several of the strange floating balls of light on film in June 2002. The photographs from their trip have been posted on the Smiths' website, where Byron has carefully taken the time to point out the orbs that he believes are genuine spirits and those that are mere accidents of light. It is because of these phenomena that the museum was chosen as the site of a large ghost research convention in 2002. Among those who attended were Janice Oberding and noted paranormal scholars Dennis William Hauck and Troy Taylor.

Even though this convention resulted in even more photographic evidence of the museum's famous orbs, no one got to see the building's most famous ghost, a full-on apparition named Miss Suzette. An on-again-off-again fixture at the school since it first closed, Miss Suzette is widely believed to be the ghost of a young teacher who taught at the school in 1908. According to the most likely version of her story, she left the school to teach at a more prestigious private institution in California, but disappeared during the journey. No one ever heard from her again until her spirit began to appear at the site of her first teaching job. How she came to be a ghost has never been explained. But her spirit has actually conversed with a handful of people over the years, most of whom were shocked to discover that the young woman in antiquated clothes was *not* an enthusiastic museum volunteer. Despite her loquaciousness, Miss Suzette has never seen fit to describe the events of her early demise, but given the psychological effects such a fate can have on a ghost, it is entirely possible that even she doesn't know how she died.

Most often seen in the schoolyard, she usually disappears from view as soon as she as reaches the front steps. Although she seems to be psychologically attached to the school, Miss Suzette has also been spotted off school grounds and on the streets close to the school. On one occasion, Lorraine and Freddie Newton came across her walking along a deserted street late at night.

"We had just moved to Virginia City, and we assumed that she was one of our neighbors," explained Lorraine. "We both thought it was weird that she was dressed in those olden-day clothes, but we had heard that there were some eccentric people around town, so we didn't say anything. She had a concerned look on her face, like she was late for something, and she was just plowing ahead at a real fast pace, so I told Freddie to drive beside her and ask her if she wanted a lift. She seemed real grateful for the offer and climbed into our backseat. It was then that I noticed that she was only about 23 or 24. I had thought she was older, because of the dress, but she was at least 10 years younger than we were. Freddie asked her where she was going, and she said the Fourth Ward School, which was strange, because even though we were new we still knew that it was a museum and not a school, and we couldn't think of a reason why someone would have to be there this late at night, but we drove her down there anyway. It wasn't a long drive, but I'm a chatty type of person, so I tried to start up a conversation, but she didn't say anything. It wasn't like she was being rude. I thought she was just shy, and I can respect that, so I didn't try to force her to talk. When we got to the museum, she got out and thanked us for the ride and walked down the school lawn to the front door. Then, and I swear I'm not making this up, she got to the front steps and just, I don't know, it was like she faded—just vanished. I'm not much for describing things, but it was like she was connected to one of those dimmer switches people sometimes have in their living rooms, and that someone turned it slowly until she wasn't there anymore. It was the strangest thing either of us have ever seen, and we've been to San Francisco five times, so that's saying a lot."

It is stories like this one that have helped Virginia City earn its reputation as a place where deceased souls stay. The Fourth Ward School is probably the most gentle and peaceful of all the schools mentioned in these pages. With the exception of Miss Suzette, none of the school's other ghosts have ever appeared in human form or have ever attempted to make their identities known, so there is little drama in this haunted school, only spirit.

A Tree Grows in Austin

METZ ELEMENTARY,
AUSTIN, TEXAS

When Joe Torres of Austin, Texas, started Torres Trucking and Excavation, he knew that there were going to be certain things he would always have to deal with. Machinery was going to break down, employees were going to get hurt, call in sick or quit and the people who hired him were always going to try and convince him that he could get things done cheaper and faster than common sense would allow. He was prepared for these things and had developed strategies to deal with them. But on occasion, something would happen that would catch him unawares. The most extreme example occurred when he was hired to demolish the Metz Elementary School. The problems he faced on this job were unlike any he had ever encountered, and he knew he was in way over his head when he found himself on the phone talking to an exorcist.

Built in East Austin in 1916, Metz Elementary by 1990 had become a safety hazard. The decision was made for a new school to be built in its place, but before construction could begin, the old school had to be torn down. Joe's company was given the contract, and just before he was to start, he toured the old school with his son Gabriel. Never a superstitious man, Joe shrugged off the strange sounds he heard as they walked through the empty place. Although he thought he heard the distinct sounds of chalk scratching on a blackboard and of children laughing and playing, he convinced himself that it was simply a matter of his memory of the sounds that he remembered from his years at school. He thought it was funny how the mind could play tricks on a person. He kept on walking, never mentioning what he heard to Gabriel, who would have informed his father that he had heard the sounds as well.

Work on the demolition began with a mass of men and machinery descending on the old school. Almost immediately, it became clear that this job wasn't going to be normal. Joe's laborers claimed that they heard strange noises coming from inside the building. Joe was shocked to hear that the descriptions these men gave matched the sounds he had heard in the school just a few days before. Then accidents started to happen. Men reported that someone or something was shaking ladders, causing them to fall and injure themselves. Soon machinery began to break down. On one day, five important pieces of equipment stopped working almost simultaneously. Joe sent a truck out to find replacement parts but its transmission blew before it returned. But it didn't matter because the mechanics Joe hired couldn't find anything wrong with the malfunctioning machines.

After that, the crewmen began to tell stories of ghosts among themselves. Joe remained skeptical, but the men were convinced and told him that they weren't going back in the school until something was done. The stoppages were costing Joe a lot of money, so he tried to think of something he could do.

Knowing little about the supernatural, he considered the few things here and there that he had come across. He remembered seeing *The Exorcist* and thought that if an exorcist could deal with the devil, he should be able to deal with some ghosts. At the Casa Guadalupe Catholic Center he found a lay evangelist named Elias Limon. Elias descended on the site with a jug of holy water and a Bible. He prayed throughout the building, asking that its restless souls be allowed to find peace. Unfortunately, his prayers were ignored.

Not long after Elias blessed the site and tried to exorcise its demons, a wall unexpectedly exploded and killed a worker. The sounds continued after that, and work at the site ground to a slow, costly crawl, taking half a year longer to complete than had originally been scheduled.

By 1992 the new Metz Elementary was completed, and the new building was free of the spirits that had been so prevalent in the old. The ghosts evidently saw no reason to stay. Now a bilingual school, the students at Metz learn in both Spanish and English and are familiar in both languages with the story of how difficult it was for their school to be built.

As for Joe, who had fought so hard against accepting any paranormal explanation for the events at the school, he took a step towards belief when he took a tree from the school's grounds and planted it in his daughter's front yard. To his amazement he discovered that from the tree, people could hear the distinct sounds of children laughing and playing.

6

Haunted by History

When a school has existed as long as those described in this chapter, it is guaranteed to have had at least one strange incident in its past. That is why we suggest that these schools are haunted by history.

Two Legends and One Fact

CENTRAL MICHIGAN UNIVERSITY,
MOUNT PLEASANT, MICHIGAN

Central Michigan University in the small city of Mount Pleasant, Michigan, is home to one of the most bizarre stories in this book. Warriner Hall is said to contain the phantom of a young woman who died in an accident so unbelievable that many people have dismissed it as a local legend, even though newspapers and university documents from the period prove that it actually happened. Some 15 feet away from the building sits a concrete pit connected to underground tunnels that have for years been linked to the supernatural. Also, in front of the hall there stands the university seal, which, according to legend, is haunted by a couple whose love was cut short by Michigan's notoriously nasty weather.

The pit, known around the university as the Warriner Pit, has been closed to students since 1996. Before then the pit was famous for being covered with strange satanic graffiti. Most assumed that the vandalism was merely the work of a bunch of head-banging adolescents, but there were many students and even some faculty members who believed that the pit actually served as a meeting place for the Church of Satan. Some even went so far as to suggest that the members of this satanic group were all brothers from a local fraternity who were joined together by more than a desire to drink beer and hit on coeds, but the rumor was obviously unfounded. For years, students used the pit as a quick means to get from their dorms to their

classes during the winter months. But after reports sur-
faced that students were becoming lost in the tunnels, and
in a few cases even reported missing, they were made off
limits. The graffiti was sandblasted off the walls, although
in some spots it is still evident, and the administration let
it be known that any student caught in the pit would be
expelled immediately. Since then there have been frequent
reports of strange sounds emanating from the pit. Usually
these eerie noises are caused by the maintenance men
who check on the pipes that travel along its tunnels, but
that hasn't stopped students from saying that the pit is

haunted by the ghosts of those who entered it and never came out.

It is unclear when the story involving the university seal first emerged. Unlike the story involving Warriner Hall, there is no evidence that this story is based on fact, but given its popularity around the campus it should not be ignored. Usually said to occur sometime during the 1950s, the story involves a young couple caught in the typical born-of-different-worlds situation. He was the rich son of an important Michigan family, and she was a poor girl, raised by her grandmother after her father went to prison for killing her mother. Appalled by her family history, his parents forbade their son from seeing her and threatened to disown him if he disobeyed them. What they failed to realize was that the choice between wealth and poverty with the love of his life wasn't a choice at all. He decided then and there to elope with his beloved and rid himself of the shallow trappings that so obsessed the rest of his family.

He called her at the restaurant where she worked and proposed to her over the phone. She accepted with a squeal of joyous delight and told him to pick her up at midnight in front of the school seal. He agreed and went back to his parents to tell them what he thought. Angered beyond reason, his father ordered him to leave their home and never return. His son slammed out of the house and left them forever. As he walked outside, he found that the winter night had grown colder than he had remembered it being. He worried that his girlfriend would get sick if she waited for him outside. He wanted to call her and tell her to meet him someplace warmer, but he couldn't go back into his parents' house. So he decided to call her on a pay phone along the way. The weather was taking a toll on his car engine, but after a few agonizing tries he managed to get it running. He drove to a nearby convenience store and called the restaurant where she worked. Unfortunately, he was told that she had just left. Worried about her welfare, he jumped back into his car and tried to start it again. This time the engine simply wouldn't turn over. As it neared midnight he frantically tried to stop passing motorists to help him jump-start his car, but no one was willing to stop in the cold weather.

His girlfriend shivered uncontrollably as she stood in front of the school seal. Her body was insistently telling her to find someplace warm, but her brain kept telling her that her boyfriend would show up at any moment. She was afraid that if she wasn't there when he arrived, he would assume that she had changed her mind.

The longest hour of the young man's life passed as he tried to find help. Finally, an older man in a pickup truck stopped, sensing how desperate the young man was. The young man thanked the man profusely and explained to him why he was so anxious. The older man listened to the boy's story and reassured him that his girlfriend would have the sense to get out of the cold. The boy thanked the man for his reassurances and for the jump-start that did indeed get his car running again. He raced down the icy roads to get to her, praying that the old man was right.

But she lost track of time as she waited for him. She knew he would come for her. She knew.

As he drove recklessly down the street, to his horror, he heard the sound of one of his back wheels popping. His car skidded into a snow bank. Tears began to stream down his face as he imagined the curse that must have been put on him to torture him this way. As fast as he could he changed the tire and got back into the car and drove just as recklessly as before to get to her.

She was so cold. So very cold.

As soon as he got to the school seal he leapt out of his car, two hours after he had agreed to meet her. She was still there, lying on the ground, her skin blue and her body immobile. For what seemed like days, but was only a few seconds, he stared at her. He felt the cold air gnaw and bite at his flesh. He could think of only one thing to do. He lay down beside her and hugged her close to him and waited.

According to the legend, these two tragic lovers met again in the spirit world. It is said that if a young couple kisses in front of the university's seal at the stroke of midnight under a full moon, then the ghosts of the young couple will join them. They will bless the couple, ensuring that they will spend the rest of their lives happily together.

Unlike the story of the seal, the story of the ghost of Warriner Hall is based on fact, even though it sounds just as fictitious. In 1937, Warriner Hall was just 10 years old, having replaced the building that had stood there previously after it had burned down in an accidental fire. A three-story, moss-covered building made of brick, the architecture of the hall includes a central tower that stands an additional two stories. As well as being the building that appears in all of the university's advertising, it is also home to the majority of the school's administrators, including the president. Back then the school was still known as the Central State Teachers' College, and one of its employees was a young woman named Theresa

Schumacher. Just 19, Theresa worked at the Warriner Hall cafeteria, and her duties included taking food to the administrators in their offices. On Saturday, May 29, she was doing just that when the elevator she was in appeared to stop between floors.

Unsure what to do next, Theresa began to randomly punch at the elevator buttons, until she noticed a small window on the elevator's door. It looked like it would open, so she tried it. It turned out that she was right, so she opened it and stuck her head out to see if she could figure out what was wrong. Unfortunately, as she did, the elevator started back up, and her head struck a bar in the shaft. For years, whenever the story was told on the campus, it was said that Theresa was decapitated, but the truth was that the elevator stopped once again, with her head wedged painfully between the bar and the window ledge. It was in this position that she slowly suffocated to death with the ledge pushing against her windpipe.

Almost immediately after her body was discovered, reports of supernatural phenomena began to surface. Lights mysteriously go on and off on the sixth floor where she died. The elevator has been known to act peculiarly, opening its doors even when no one has pressed the call buttons, closing them quickly when someone tries to step inside, and stopping and starting suddenly for no reason.

Back in the 1960s, when the hall still housed the campus radio station, the late-night deejay was sorting some albums when he heard the elevator start and the doors open. Having assumed that he was alone in the building, he turned to see who was there. His jaw dropped when he saw the apparition of a girl in an antiquated cafeteria

uniform standing in the middle of the elevator. Even from afar he could see the dark purple bruise that ran all the way around her neck. Before he could say or do anything, the elevator doors closed. He never saw her again, even though he kept the unpopular shift on the off chance that he might.

The stories that involve Central Michigan's Warriner Hall are all normal examples of the kinds of stories that attach themselves to the more imposing buildings that sit on North American campuses. The stories involving the infamous pit and the university seal are most probably fictitious, but they are still interesting. The story of the Warriner ghost, on the other hand, has a firm basis in reality, even though it sounds just as fantastic as the others, proving that often the difference between reality and fiction isn't as obvious as many people would assume.

Ghosts of the Ivy League

HARVARD, PRINCETON AND YALE

When North America's smartest and most ambitious students dream of the university that will most dramatically ensure that their lives will be filled with nothing but honor and riches, it is guaranteed that the school they imagine will be on the east coast of the United States and that ivy grows on the sides of its buildings. Whether it's Harvard, Princeton or Yale, everyone who applies to these schools does so because they believe that being accepted will be the first step in a life devoted to excellence. And that is because the schools themselves believe it. The schools of the Ivy League have become so used to the idea that they set the standard for academic achievement throughout the world, that they are loath to admit that they might graduate someone not destined for greatness. Harvard, for example, takes its cue from the British universities Oxford and Cambridge, and refuses to admit that one of its students might fail a class. Instead of receiving an F, a student who does poorly in a class is given a "gentleman's pass." The only reason these universities can risk this sort of arrogance is that time and again they have been proven right.

With Harvard and Yale having been around for over three centuries and Princeton for two and a half, it seems natural that over the years they have amassed a collection of distinguished alumni. But they have also collected some of the spirits of the people whose lives were somehow touched by those alumni.

Located in the town of Princeton, New Jersey, Princeton University was founded in 1746. Since then it has had no less than two former U.S. presidents (James Madison, class of 1771, and Woodrow Wilson, class of 1879) serve as

Princeton's president and was the home of quite possibly the most famous scientist of the 20th century, Albert Einstein. Its most famous ghost is a former student named Hamilton Murray. Hamilton graduated from the university in 1872. A boyish-looking man with long sideburns and a dour expression, he died a year after he graduated when the ship he sailed on was lost during a terrible storm. Six years later, his family donated enough money for a school building to be built in his name. A dark gray stone building of short but imposing stature, Murray Hall, was later joined to nearby Dodge Hall by a cloister and renamed Murray-Dodge Hall. Inside the Murray side of the building is a theater that serves as home for the student repertory company, Theater Intime. It is here that Hamilton's spirit is said to reside. Tools have been known to disappear and reappear on stage, along with props and pieces of scenery, and the figure of a young man in a long coat and top hat has been spotted for the briefest of seconds on the side of the stage during many dress rehearsals. Also, in the hall just outside the theater, students have reported that the framed photograph of Hamilton that hangs there often glows mysteriously. On some occasions the glow is so bright that the picture can be seen in an otherwise pitch-black room.

Of the three famous schools, Yale seems to have had the most humble beginnings. Founded in 1701 as the Collegiate School in the Killingworth, Connecticut, home of Abraham Pierson, the school moved to New Haven 15 years later after receiving a generous gift from Elihu Yale. The school was renamed in 1718. Since then the school has grown in both size and prominence until it took its place as one of the most prestigious schools in the world. Among its famous alumni are the last three American presidents, George Bush, Bill Clinton and George W. Bush.

Yale's most famous ghost resides in immaculate Woolsey Hall. This auditorium was built in 1901 and was named after the school's former president Theodore Woolsey. Home to one of the world's largest pipe organs, the hall is haunted by Professor Harry Jepson, a music teacher at Yale who composed many of the hymns that were performed in the school's Battell Chapel during the 20s and 30s. Despite the presence of the Newbury Memorial Organ, Professor Jepson loathed the large hall, preferring instead the intimacy of the school's small chapel. He refused even to enter the hall, even though several of his compositions were played there. After he died it became apparent that his spirit had had a change of heart and could not deny itself the sounds of the large, romantic organ. Late at night the sounds of his music can be heard echoing throughout the building he once reviled.

Harvard, which at the end of the millennium celebrated its 364th birthday, is the oldest institution of higher learning in the United States. Among the men who at one point walked along its campus on their way to class are Teddy Roosevelt and Franklin Roosevelt, John Quincy Adams and John F. Kennedy. The school was established in 1636 and was named after John Harvard, a young minister whose untimely death in 1638 made him the school's first benefactor. Built on half of what had been John's estate in what would become the college town of Cambridge, Massachusetts, the school grew to become a

powerful academic institution. Over the years the campus grew and soon claimed buildings that had once served other purposes. One of these buildings, Thayer Hall, was originally a textile mill before it was taken over by the university. A large five-story building made of red brick, the hall is a thoroughly unremarkable building save for one fact—the grounds around it are haunted by the spirits of former workers who can be seen at night trying to return to the mill where they once worked. Dressed in period clothing, these apparitions have been seen floating around the entrances, apparently stopped by some mysterious force from going inside. The building that exists today is slightly different than these ghosts remember it, and as a result, they can also be seen hovering around places where doors once were. As yet no one has been able to adequately explain why these spirits are so connected to the building. It has been suggested that many mills of the period were dangerous workplaces and may have claimed the lives of many workers, but there is no evidence to prove the theory. Once thick and plentiful, the ghosts are much more rarely seen now that artificial lights have been placed around the perimeter of the building. But reports of their appearances still occur, especially during the winter months when the heat indoors becomes an added incentive for them to come inside.

As academic institutions, Harvard, Princeton and Yale have long stood at the head of the class. With their impressive histories and long lists of famous alumni, it isn't any wonder that they can claim to house their share of school spirits. Their ghosts are not as impressive or unique as others that appear in this book, but the spirits at least have a certain dignity coming from schools of their status.

Taking Care of Hillhurst

Jessica Mason (not her real name) had been a teacher at Hillhurst School in Calgary, Alberta, for four years, when she walked into the school an hour before classes and saw the floating gray figure of the man whose picture hung in the school's main hallway. He didn't say a word to her, and she didn't say anything to him. Although blind terror and a loud scream on her part wouldn't have been unreasonable reactions, Jessica chose instead to just nod and smile at the elderly spirit. She walked past him and into the school office. It was still quite early, so she was the only person there. She looked around and found the large notebook that was reserved for recording events of the day. She opened it up to the first blank page, penciled in the date and wrote "saw ghost this morning." When the rest of the school staff began to arrive at work, they noticed the open logbook and looked at what she had written.

"Was he doing anything this time?" asked the principal.

"Nope," Jessica admitted. "He was just standing there."

"Who was?" asked the school's secretary, as she walked into the office.

"Stevie," answered the principal.

"Ahh," nodded the secretary, who didn't need to hear anymore.

Anyone who took the time to go through the school logbook would discover that "saw ghost this morning" was a note that appeared frequently throughout its pages. Hillhurst had been haunted for years, but its resident ghost was so benign that, after the original shock wore off, its appearances hardly raised an eyebrow anymore. In the logbook the first descriptions of ghostly encounters were long, involved affairs with detailed notes about every relevant factor, but as the months passed, the descriptions grew shorter and shorter until "saw ghost this morning" pretty much said it all. At this rate, it wouldn't be long before people would simply write the word "ghost" after an encounter, and then eventually do away with the effort of writing an entire word and just write the letter "g."

It's a hard to believe that a school would become so blasé about something so extraordinary, but no matter how strange or special something is, once you've seen it for the nth time, it's hard to get excited about it. Especially when all Hillhurst's ghost ever did was make the occasional appearance or, when invisible, cause the hallway doors open and close as if by themselves. No one really wanted him to become violent or scary, but many would have liked it if he at least did something interesting. The problem was that Stevie hadn't even been interesting when he was alive.

Ernest Stevenson had been a caretaker at the school. He had actually lived at the school, in a room on the third floor, and he had taken his job very seriously. Much beloved at the school because of his dedication and patience, Ernest was one who saw his position as caretaker not as means to a paycheck, but as a calling. In much the same way that a captain becomes dedicated to his boat or a head chef to his kitchen, it isn't uncommon for a school caretaker to form a special and unique bond with the building that has been entrusted to his care.

Ernest loved the school, and it genuinely pained him to see it in anything less than pristine condition. It wasn't uncommon for him to spend hours dusting and cleaning nooks and crannies that no one ever looked in, just on the off chance that someone might. Ernest would have been deeply ashamed if anyone ever found even a speck of dirt in his school. He had to be constantly vigilant in his fight against the natural tendency to disorder that any building faces daily, and as a result, he wasn't the most interesting person to be around. To strike up a conversation with Ernest inevitably led to a discussion of how much work he had to do and how little time he had to do it, even though, since he lived at school, his working hours were only limited by how much time he needed to eat or sleep.

It isn't surprising then, that when he died he couldn't bring himself to leave the place where he had invested so much of his life. What is surprising is that one of the few staff members who has yet to see his ghost is the man who currently does his job. Doug Wolfe, the present care-taker, has only the word of his colleagues that Stevie actu-ally exists, which suggests that either the old ghost is too polite to bother a fellow caretaker or that it doesn't want to admit that Hillhurst is in someone else's hands.

Hillhurst is unique among the schools in this book, because it takes care to acknowledge and document its ghost's existence while doing absolutely nothing about it. No one has ever tried to hold a séance or perform an exorcism or do anything that might change the status quo, and for the moment, there is no reason to do so. Stevie stays at the school because it's his home, and he treats it that way, refusing to disturb anybody by taking part in any of the more stereotypical phantom activities. As long as he keeps quiet and stays boring, then the only thing that will ever happen when he appears is another note in the school logbook.

For Reference Only

DEPAUW UNIVERSITY, GREENCASTLE, INDIANA

Greencastle, Indiana, is a sleepy little college town just 45 minutes away from Indianapolis, where it has served as home to Depauw University since 1837. It is not the sort of place that one would expect to find a ghost, because it is almost completely free of the scandal and melodrama that so often go hand in hand with the supernatural. As well, Depauw's emphasis on academics has kept most students too busy to become involved in the type of shenanigans recounted in this book. As a consequence, there are no ghosts of despairing suicides, murdered lovers, dead pledges or disgruntled staff members creeping along its corridors. But in keeping with the school's nose-to-the-grindstone ethos, there *is* a collection of haunted books.

"Boy, if you don't stop reading those useless books, you'll never learn how to turn a crop, then I guarantee that you will never amount to anything for anybody."

In 1843, 37 years after James Whitcomb's father made this pronouncement, his son was elected Indiana's eighth governor. Over the years, James never did learn how to turn a crop, and he spent every spare second reading and learning everything he could from the books he loved so

dearly, proving to his father that your hands need not be callused for you to be successful. A lawyer by trade, he got his start in politics when Indiana's then-governor James B. Ray appointed him as the fifth district's prosecuting attorney. Four years later he was elected to the state senate, where he served six consecutive terms. He then spent two terms as Indiana's governor, as well as a term in the U.S. senate, before he died in 1852. During the 57 years that he lived, he amassed a great collection of books, many of which were rare and extremely valuable. Not wanting his collection to be sold or broken up, he decided to leave the books to Depauw's well-respected library. He made it clear that the books were to be used for reference only and that they should never be allowed to be taken out. The university happily agreed to his terms and out of gratitude named their library after him, not knowing how serious Governor Whitcomb was when he wrote the clause into his will.

For the next 40 years, the books were treated with great care, and the librarians were strict in their adherence to their benefactor's wishes. The books were used strictly for research and were never removed from the premises, that is until one volume captured the imagination of one young student.

Cedric was every bit the bookworm that Governor Whitcomb was. He took in books as naturally and easily as most people eat, sleep and breathe. The Whitcomb Library was easily his favorite place in the world, and he spent hours every day going through its books. His goal was to have read every book by the time he had graduated. To most people reading that many books would seem an insurmountably daunting task, but to Cedric it was as close as a living mortal could come to heaven. He only wished that the library wouldn't close so early. He hated that every night he would inevitably feel the librarian tap him on his shoulder to tell him that it was time to go, just as what he was reading really got interesting. Often he thought about hiding whatever book he was reading underneath his shirt and finishing it at home.

For two semesters he had managed to fight the temptation, until one night he picked up a dusty tome entitled *The Poems of Oisín*. Originally written in India and published in Philadelphia in 1789, the book of exotic verse had been given to Governor Whitcomb on his 18th birthday and had held a special place in his heart. Cedric had never encountered anything like it before. Even translated into English, its poems seemed foreign and mysterious. Each one was more enigmatic than the next, causing Cedric's mind to jump and swerve and double-back as it tried to work out their meanings. He was only a quarter of the way through when he felt the dreaded tap on his shoulder. It was all he could do to stop himself from screaming. He couldn't stop now! He was just beginning to understand what he was reading!

For the first time in his life, Cedric decided that there was no choice but to break the rules. The very thought of it made his heart pound and his pulse race. His face turned beet red and his hands shook as he looked around and waited for the right moment to commit his crime. As soon as he was sure that no one was watching him, he hid the book underneath his shirt. He tried his best to calm down and managed to make it out of the library. Once he was outside, he slipped the book out from under his shirt and ran to his dorm room as fast as he could. He slammed his door behind him and was so excited by what he had done that he had to wait 15 minutes before he could calm himself down enough to start reading again.

Over the next three hours he finished the book, taking time to read over each poem more than once as he strove to understand it. Once he was satisfied he put on his nightclothes, slipped the book under his pillow, turned off his light and went to sleep.

As he dreamed of exotic warriors and mysterious Indian locales, his room was infused with a musty odor. It was strong enough to awaken him from his reverie. As he lay in his bed, with his left cheek on his pillow, he heard what sounded like someone in his room.

"Who's there?" he muttered groggily, not completely sure that he wasn't still dreaming.

A series of slow heavy footsteps made their way to the end of his bed. With a groan, Cedric turned and sat up to see who was there. He was met by a furious roar and a blinding flash of white light.

"Thief!" shouted the decrepit figure at the foot of his bed. "That is not your book!"

All the blood drained from Cedric's face as he realized he was looking at the ghost of James Whitcomb.

"*Oison* is mine! Return it at once!" the skeletal figure ordered, pointing its bony index figure at the terrified young man.

"Yes sir!" Cedric shouted back. "Whatever you say!"

"At once!"

Cedric leapt from his bed and grabbed the purloined book from beneath his pillow. Still dressed in his night-clothes, he ran out of his room and hotfooted it over to the library, which wouldn't be open for another four hours. Too afraid to return to his room, Cedric hugged the book to his chest and sat, rocking back and forth, at the library door. Finally, the morning librarian arrived. She was a little surprised to find an ashen-faced young man sitting at the door. As soon as he saw her, he thrust the book into her hands.

"I'm sorry!" he apologized. "I'll never do it again! I promise!"

With that he left the dumbfounded librarian and ran back to his room where, having completed his task, he promptly fainted.

When he awoke from where he had fallen on the floor, he decided that books were too dangerous to trifle with. When he got up, he got dressed and went to the administration building and told them what had happened that night. With that said, he informed them that he was leaving the school because he had decided to take up the less hazardous profession of farming, which he did with some success.

As word of the governor's unexpected appearance spread around campus, at least one student was seen racing towards the library with a pilfered book, obviously afraid that she would receive a similar visit. After that incident, the librarians found it very easy to keep the governor's books inside the library.

School Spirit

There are two very different attitudes a school can adopt when faced with the possibility that it is haunted. The most typical response is stout denial, which makes sense when it comes to a place where parents are expected to feel safe about sending their children. Unlike haunted hotels, theaters or houses, there is little prestige in being a haunted school, as the ghosts inside them are often reminders of incidents that the faculty would prefer to be forgotten. The other possible response, acceptance and approval, is less likely to be found. But there are some schools that are not only at peace with their ghosts, but who take pride in them as well.

Since 1956, the staff and students at Galt Collegiate High School in Cambridge, Ontario, have honored their well-publicized phantoms by nicknaming their various sports teams the Ghosts and by giving the term "school spirit" a more significant meaning than it would have at any other school. Founded in 1853 by Dr. William Tassie, Galt Collegiate is the oldest continuously operated high school in Ontario. Built in the spooky gothic style popular during the period, the building has not one, but two seven-story towers, giving the school a slightly ominous façade, a feeling that is quickly dispelled by the grace and good humor of its faculty and students.

With a student population of 1250, it isn't any wonder that the school's various ghosts avoid the daytime, as their ethereal efforts would be invariably drowned out by the

sights and sounds of rambunctious teenagers. They wait for night, where they can be seen, heard and smelled without having to compete with other distractions.

The light outside had turned to twilight as Jen Cole walked into one of the girls' washrooms one evening in 1999. A peer counselor, Jen had stayed late after classes to meet with some students who needed help. Inside the washroom she heard what she thought was one of the students she had just talked to. The meeting had obviously touched an emotional chord for the student as Jen listened to her weep from inside a stall. Jen's first instinct was to knock on the stall door and try to comfort the girl, but she didn't want to invade the girl's privacy, especially in the washroom where people tend to be at their most vulnerable. Knowing that one of her friends was outside in the hall, Jen popped her head out of the bathroom door and got her attention.

"There's a girl crying in here," she said. "What do you think I should do?"

Jen's friend hesitated, as she mulled over the same points that had caused Jen to ask the question in the first place.

"You should talk to her," Jen's friend finally decided. "Bad things could happen if she's left alone."

Jen nodded her head and went back into the washroom. The girl had stopped crying and the room was filled with an uncomfortable silence. Jen went over to the stall from which the crying had come, and knocked softly on the door.

"Are you okay in there?" she asked quietly.

The force of her light taps moved the door just enough to indicate that the stall door wasn't latched. Jen cautiously pushed it open and saw that the stall was now empty.

Jen swung her head around the small washroom to see if the girl had left the stall while she had popped her head outside. The room looked empty. Jen checked the other stalls to make sure she hadn't tried the wrong one and found that they too were vacant. To Jen's wide-eyed shock and amazement, she realized that she was the only person in the room. She had been in this washroom many times, and she knew that there was only one way out, the door at which she had stood to get advice from her friend. The bathroom had been empty the whole time.

Over the past three years, no one has been able to identify the spirit whose painful sobs Jen heard that day. Whoever she is, she is just one of many ghosts who manifest themselves inside the school. Of these phantoms, just two have been identified as being firmly connected to the school's past. The first of these is the school's founder and first principal, Dr. William Tassie. Night custodian Ralph Bullock, who attended Galt Collegiate in the 70s, knows that Dr. Tassie is near whenever he smells the distinct odor of pipe tobacco in the air. One of the only former members of the school's faculty to smoke a pipe, Dr. Tassie is believed to haunt the school because of the way he had been forced out of it. An ardent misogynist, Dr. Tassie refused to allow girls to be taught at the school he had founded. By 1881, however, local demands made his position untenable, and Dr. Tassie was given an ultimatum: allow girls to be taught at Galt or tender his resignation. He chose the latter.

Ralph has had several encounters with Dr. Tassie over the years. During one weekend, he found three doors he had thought to be closed and locked, wide open. When he went to close them, he found that the doorknobs were indeed still locked, making it difficult to explain how they could have been opened, especially since he was the only person in the building. On another weekend, he looked down while cleaning a window and saw two shadows on the floor instead of one. Right beside his was a cloudy shape that faded away almost as soon as he noticed it.

The strangest incidents involving Dr. Tassie are the continued disappearances of stockings and nylons from the girls' locker room. Even though padlocks protect all the lockers, these undergarments routinely vanish. The popular explanation is that the still-bitter Dr. Tassie is trying to send a message to the school's female population that he considers them unwelcome.

The second of the school's identified ghosts is that of David MacGeorge, a bushy-bearded Scotsman who was one of the school's most popular custodians as well as a published poet. He actually lived at the school for 40 years until his death in 1925. A collection of his verses, entitled *Ae' Glint on Ither Days* is still kept in the school library. Its presence in the school is what many believe keeps the gregarious Scot inside his former home. Never as menacing or as foul tempered as Dr. Tassie, David's presence is most often indicated instead by a feeling of warmth and safety, the same feeling he lent to the school when he was still alive.

The ghosts of Galt Collegiate are nothing to be ashamed of. By acknowledging and honoring the presence of its spirits, the staff proves that an institution of learning need not hide behind a cloak of denial when it comes to the supernatural. By embracing the past, they allow for a richer atmosphere in which their students can more easily connect to the history that so often feels distant and unexceptional. Perhaps Galt Collegiate serves as the model for what every haunted school should aim to be.

Ivan's Best Friend

UNIVERSITY OF TORONTO,
TORONTO, ONTARIO

With a total of 53,000 students and 11,000 faculty and staff members, the University of Toronto has a larger population than many of the cities mentioned in other stories in this book. It is, not surprisingly, the largest school in Canada, encompassing three campuses on the east, west and center of Toronto. It is also one of Canada's oldest schools, having been given its Royal Charter in 1827, although classes didn't actually begin until 1843. But its history and its size are not its only distinctions. Unlike the majority of universities in North America, the University of Toronto is not a single entity unto itself. The school follows the tradition set by the British universities of Oxford and Cambridge and is made up of 12 federated colleges (University, Victoria, Trinity, St. Michael's, Knox, Wycliffe, Erindale, New, Innis, Scarborough, Massey and Woodsworth). The separate colleges allow for a greater independence among the different fields of study and a greater number of students.

Having 12 separate colleges also means having as many buildings to house them, and it is these buildings that also bring distinction to the university. The buildings were all constructed over the course of 175 years, and it comes as no shock that they all represent varying periods of architectural style. To look at them is to instantly be aware of how old some are in comparison to others. The building that houses University College is one of the oldest. A large gothic building made of dark gray brick, it looks as though it would have been the perfect setting for a novel by one of the Brontë sisters. An intricate length of wrought iron sits atop the roof, which is eclipsed by the occasional tower and spire, in a touch that lends credence to the gut feeling that University College is not a place where it is easy to be comfortable. Everything about it is hard, heavy and sharp, an apt metaphor for what it can feel like to have the weight of an education put in your lap.

"Is that place haunted?" is a question commonly asked by students and visitors when they first see the imposing structure. If the person they are with knows anything about the history of the school, then the answer is, "Yes, it is."

University College was first established in 1853, but three years later construction on the building had only just begun. The project was ambitious and required a large assortment of skilled laborers, many of whom had just arrived in Canada. Among the most vital of these were the stonemasons, who counted in their number two Russians. Both Ivan Reznikoff and Paul Diablos were literally "just off the boat" when they were hired to work on the college. Despite their common ancestry and profession, both men could not have been more different. Ivan was a monster of a man, standing 6' 5" and weighing just over 300 pounds, and Paul was almost a foot shorter and 150 pounds lighter. Ivan's face was prematurely aged from years of cold weather and hard work, which he tried to hide with a bushy beard and mustache. Paul, on the other hand, was handsome. He too wore a mustache, but his was always neat and well groomed in the style of the Russian aristocracy, which was ironic given the effort he made to distance

himself from his country of birth. Ivan was proud to be Russian and it never occurred to him that his foreign-sounding name might work against him, but Paul was much more cautious. Hoping to avoid discrimination, he changed his name, choosing Paul from the Bible he had used to learn English and Diablos from a suggestion made by a friend, who thought the Spanish word for devil more than accurately described the roguish lothario.

Despite, or maybe because of, their differences the two men became fast friends and worked together side by side. Ivan was a quiet man who had done little socializing in his life, so he enjoyed listening to the stories Paul told about the parties he went to and the women he had known. Paul encouraged the large man to come out of his shell and helped him with his English. Thanks to Paul's efforts, Ivan now had the confidence to become a part of Toronto's social scene. He shaved off the beard, but kept the mustache and went to dances and recitals and any other place where he could meet people. It was at a dance where he met a British woman named Susie. At first, Ivan was too scared to approach the beautiful blonde, because he was certain that she would be frightened by his stature, but then he began to notice her looking his way and soon got the impression that she was waiting for him to introduce himself. Incredibly nervous, the big man took a deep breath, walked over to her and introduced himself with his heavily accented English.

To his shock and surprise, the pretty young woman didn't run away from him. Instead, she giggled, introduced herself and strongly hinted that if he wanted to dance, all he had to do was ask. He asked, and from that moment on they were inseparable. For the next several months Paul was subjected to Ivan's enthusiastic descriptions of Susie's every action. It amused him to see his friend so smitten, although secretly he wondered if Ivan was being a bit too generous in his depiction of the young woman. It was hard for him to believe that a woman as beautiful as Ivan described would be interested in the bearish Russian.

One morning as they started working, Paul couldn't help but notice the huge smile on his friend's face.

"I have never seen you so happy," he noted. "Did your Susie give you a kiss last night?" he teased.

"Better!" Ivan beamed.

"Better than a kiss? I can't think of such a thing." Paul enjoyed having fun with Ivan's innocent nature. He could certainly think of many things that would be better than a kiss.

"Paul," Ivan stood straight up and addressed his friend, "I want you be the first to hear. Me and my Susie, we are getting married."

Paul looked at Ivan and saw that his friend spoke the truth. He stopped what he was doing and gave his friend a big hug.

"Congratulations! Congratulations!" he enthused.

"I want you to meet her," Ivan said after they finished hugging. "I want her to know my greatest friend."

"Of course, I must meet her," Paul smiled. "We will go out and celebrate together tonight."

That night Ivan introduced his fiancée to his best friend. Paul was amazed to find that Susie was every bit as beautiful as Ivan had described. He could not believe his oafish friend had captured such a wonderful prize. He was not the only one who was taken aback. Over the past couple of months, Susie had heard many stories about Ivan's handsome friend who worked beside him at the college construction site, but she had difficulty accepting that a stonemason could ever look and act like the way Ivan had described. Now, she saw that Ivan had been telling the truth.

Overjoyed to have his two favorite people together at last, Ivan shone with a pride he had never felt before. His

pride shone so brightly that it blinded him, making it impossible for him to see the obvious attraction that was developing between Paul and Susie. During the three hours they spent together that night, Ivan never noticed that Paul and Susie were falling in love.

At first, Paul felt enormous guilt and shame over his feelings for his best friend's betrothed, but that did not stop him from going and seeing her behind Ivan's back. As the days passed, his guilt transformed itself into hatred. Why, he wondered, should a dumb giant be allowed to marry this princess, when he, a fine gentleman, was there for her to have? Paul lost all respect for his friend and, as he worked on the high tower, he found himself creating a gargoyle in the image of Ivan.

Ivan never found out that the gargoyle Paul was working on was meant to be him, but he wasn't as clueless or naive as his friend believed. He did not tell Paul that he suspected that Susie was not being true to him and that he planned to spy on her that night. He waited a long time before he saw her sneak out of the building where she lived. It was so late. Ivan had never considered it possible to be awake at this hour, but he managed not to fall asleep where he stood, and he followed her to the construction site where he worked. From a distance he watched as she met with her lover and passionately kissed him. When he saw the man she was kissing, Ivan could not believe it. To be dishonored by a stranger was one thing, but to be cuckolded by his best friend was too much for Ivan. Seeing red, Ivan screamed with rage, picked up a heavy ax and ran towards the couple.

Susie and Paul heard the scream echo in the darkness. Susie had no idea where it came from, but Paul knew immediately. He told Susie to run back home and that he would meet her later. A bit confused, she did as she was told and left Paul alone to await the arrival of his friend. He didn't have to wait long. Bellowing oaths of damnation, Ivan appeared out of the darkness, swinging his deadly ax. Paul could tell right away that there was nothing for him to say to ease Ivan's anger, so he turned and ran. Without realizing it, he found himself heading towards the tower where he had forever immortalized his friend. As he reached the tower door, Ivan caught up with him and swung his ax at Paul's head. He just barely missed, catching the ax in the door instead. Paul ran inside the tower, while Ivan tried to remove his ax from the door. Paul didn't make it far inside before Ivan grabbed at him. From inside his jacket, Paul pulled out a small knife. He turned quickly and stabbed it into his best friend's stomach. Ivan was too surprised to make a sound. He let go of Paul and looked down at blood that was pouring out of his gut. Dazed, he took a step back. His foot slipped on the top step and he fell to the bottom of the stairs with a fatal thud. Paul ran down to the body of his friend and worked out a plan for what he had to do next.

That morning Ivan did not come in to work, nor the morning after. When a week passed, it was assumed that something had happened to the big man. Nobody gave the matter much thought, and within a few months, his name was never mentioned again and no one said a word when Paul and Susie got married.

A decade passed before clues of what happened to Ivan Reznikoff began to appear. A professor named Falconbridge reported seeing the apparition of a large man floating wordlessly in the college tower. No one had any idea what to make of this event nor of the several others that occurred over the next 24 years. It wasn't until 1890 that the identity of the tower's ghost was discovered by accident. A student carrying a kerosene lamp slipped on the tower stairs and dropped it, causing a fire that did a great deal of damage to the interior. It was during the subsequent repair that a skeleton was found embedded in the college wall. Found inside its tattered clothes was a letter written in broken English to a woman named Susie by a man named Ivan. In it he claimed that she was not being faithful to him. By then Paul and Susie had long since moved away from Toronto and Ivan's murder was never avenged.

Even though his body was found and given a decent burial, Ivan's spirit remained in the tower. Students, visitors and academics could see him, always with the same look of disbelief and disappointment on his face. He can be seen there still waiting, perhaps for the man and the woman who hurt him so badly to return and apologize for what they did.

The End

GHOST HOUSE

GHOST HOUSE BOOKS

These fun, fascinating collections from GHOST HOUSE BOOKS reveal the diversity of haunted places across North Ameria. Our ghostly tales involve well-known buildings and other landmarks, many of which are still in use. Collect the whole series!

Ghost Stories of America, Volume II by A.S. Mott
Covering every region and era, A.S. Mott explores the nation's most infamous spirits, paranormal phenomena and haunted places, making this collection essential reading for skeptics and believers alike.
$10.95US/$14.95CDN • ISBN 1-894877-31-4 • 5.25" x 8.25" • 248 pages

Haunted Highways by Dan Asfar
Lights on the road. Ghost hitchhikers. Eerie covered bridges. Dan Asfar shows how some of America's most innocuous streets and thoroughfares can suddenly become terrifying haunts.
$10.95US/$14.95CDN • ISBN 1-894877-29-2 • 5.25" x 8.25" • 224 pages

Haunted Houses by Edrick Thay
With their blend of captivating history and ethereal residents, haunted houses have long been considered the most exciting haunted places. This eagerly awaited collection reveals why.
$10.95US/$14.95CDN • ISBN 1-894877-30-6 • 5.25" x 8.25" • 256 pages

Ghost Stories of the Old West by Dan Asfar
The OK Corral, Fort Leavenworth, Billy the Kid, the Pony Express—the old West had it all. Join Dan Asfar as he uncovers the charismatic ghosts who inhabit the prisons, forts and saloons where the West was born—and died.
$10.95US/$14.95CDN • ISBN 1-894877-17-9 • 5.25" x 8.25" • 232 pages

Also look for
Haunted Hotels *by Jo-Anne Christensen*   ISBN 1-894877-03-9
Haunted Theaters *by Barbara Smith*   ISBN 1-894877-04-7
Campfire Ghost Stories *by Jo-Anne Christensen*
                                                       ISBN 1-894877-02-0

These and many more Ghost House books are available from your local bookseller or by ordering direct. U.S. readers call 1-800-518-3541. In Canada, call 1-800-661-9017.